ARE YOU
FOCUSING
ON THE
RIGHT THING FOR
RETIREMENT?

DAVID COMPTON AND
JOHN COMPTON

Printed in the United States of America

First Printing, 2015

Gradient Positioning Systems, LLC
4105 Lexington Avenue North, Suite 110
Arden Hills, MN 55126 (877) 901-0894

Contributors: Nick Stovall, Nate Lucius, Mike Binger and Gradient Positioning Systems, LLC.

TABLE OF CONTENTS

INTRODUCTION

A man and his wife owned a very special goose. Every day the goose would lay a golden egg, which made the couple very rich.

"Just think," said the man's wife, "If we could have all the golden eggs that are inside the goose, we could be richer much faster."

"You're right," said her husband, "We wouldn't have to wait for the goose to lay her egg."

So, the couple killed the goose and cut her open, only to find that she was just like every other goose. She had no golden eggs inside of her at all, and because they had killed the goose, they no longer had the golden eggs to rely on.

Aesop's classic fable, The Goose that Laid the Golden Eggs, gives us surprising insight into the perils of retirement planning. The savings you have built up during your working years is like the goose in our story. She lays the golden eggs just as your savings, whether in an IRA, company stocks or 401(k) plan, are expected to produce the income you need during your retirement years. Will the goose of your savings be able to generate enough income? Can she continue to lay those golden eggs well into the future you have imagined for yourself?

Well, that depends on how well you take care of your goose. A well fed and protected bird no doubt has a better chance of producing more golden eggs for a longer period of time. Leaving her out all night with the coyotes and wolves puts her at risk. Many retirees are worried about outliving their savings and this is a real concern given today's longer life expectancy. Today's seniors can expect to live longer than their parents did—19 years longer for men and 15 years longer for women according to the Social Security Administration.* That combined with the rising cost of health care, inflation and the likelihood of increasing taxes and it's no wonder so many retirees are worried about running out of golden eggs. They get so worried about those golden eggs, however, they forget to take care of the goose.

CHANGING YOUR FOCUS: WHY YOU WANT TO SAVE THE GOOSE

While our goose analogy is a somewhat simplified version of things, the problem of income generation during retirement requires a different kind of thinking when it comes to the treatment of your investments. The success of your retirement depends on it. Today's cost of living, market volatility and a more spend-crazy mindset have jeopardized the stability of retirement income, along with the fact that pensions have fallen by the wayside. Fewer and fewer people are retiring with defined benefit plans like their parents did and more and more of us have to create our own plans using the retirement savings we've managed to accumulate.

---

* *http://www.ncbi.nlm.nih.gov/books/NBK62373/*

Because the focus of the investor up to this point has been on accumulating and stockpiling money, their focus as they get ready to retire tends to remain on growth. Staying focused on the rate of return—or on how many golden eggs their investments can produce—usually means forgetting about the health of the goose. In order to prepare for a successful retirement, a shift in the way you approach investing needs to happen during the years just prior to and during retirement. As you go from the accumulation stage of life to the payout or income phase, you want to change the way you look at your money. **Now is the time to refocus the lens on your binoculars and look at what your savings is actually there for.** When you are depending on the account value of your 401(k) or IRA to provide income, your focus shouldn't be on the rate of return, but rather on the safety of your principal. It's not about how big the pot is, but about the pot's ability to generate income for you, now and in the future. In a 2014 article written for the Harvard Business Review called "The Crisis in Retirement Planning," economist Robert C. Merton describes it this way:

"Investment decisions are now focused on the value of the funds, the returns on investment they deliver, and how volatile those returns are. Yet the primary concern of the saver remains what it always has been: Will I have sufficient income in retirement to live comfortably?"

Maintaining a comfortable lifestyle during retirement depends on the ability of your savings to generate a comfortable income. Not taking care of your goose is the equivalent of not protecting the principal of those retirement savings. Your principal is your base amount, the money you have earned that you have right now, sitting in the bank or in various investment accounts. The larger than principal, the more income it can generate. Do you know what kind of risk those investments are exposed to? Are those returns guaranteed? Is your principal protected? Exposing your principal to the risk of stock market volatility means one thing: you risk cooking your goose.

And no goose means no more golden eggs.

WHAT WILL THE SUCCESS OF YOUR RETIREMENT DEPEND ON?

The number one mistake most retirees make today is not securing their income. **Even though today's seniors are independent and knowledgeable and want the choice of retiring on their own terms, when they expose too much money to risk, that choice is taken away from them.** When you rely on market investments and venture capital for income production and the market is up, you might feel good, but this is a false sense of security because when the market tanks, you significantly reduce your ability to sustain that income. Do you want the success of your retirement based on market timing that you have no control over? Or do you want the peace of mind that comes from knowing your retirement income has been secured?

Study after study reveals that most Americans fear outliving their money. There is a way to make sure this doesn't happen to you. When you change your focus from maximizing returns to the task of maximizing income, the investment tools and strategies you need also change. There are investment products and strategies designed to give you the guarantees you need when retiring during today's unpredictable economic climate. These investment tools can position your principal in a safe, conservative portfolio while also giving you opportunity. What we mean by opportunity is the chance for growth. We're not relegating your dollar down to bond and CD rates because that can be just as dangerous to the longevity of your savings. The investment products we recommend and the strategies we use for income creation can still give you golden eggs indexed to market performance while also protecting and caring for your goose. This is what we mean when we say, "*safety and opportunity on the same dollar, at the same time*." These golden eggs may or may not be as big and shiny, but they keep on coming and they don't have an expiration date.

OUR APPROACH TO INCOME SECURITY

When making smart investment choices that will affect your income security, we believe it's imperative to identify first what it is you need your money to do for you. **The purpose of the money dictates how it should be positioned.** Different financial tools are designed to do different things. Some investment tools are designed for growth, others for protection, and still others can do a little bit of both. Checking and savings accounts provide you with liquid funds to pay the bills; life insurance can protect your loved ones and build a legacy; accounts earmarked for accumulation such as 401(k), 403(b) or IRAs grow money for your retirement years. Once you begin the transition into retirement, you need financial tools that protect your principal, grow your money and provide an income for you, either now or a few years down the road.

Because understanding whether or not an investment is right for you begins with understanding what it is you want your money to do, our approach to income planning begins with your individual goals. From there, we have a conversation about risk tolerance and whether or not the investments you have are in fact aligned with your current objectives. There are a lot of common misperceptions out there about investment products and terms. As the financial industry continues to respond to the needs of retirees, it comes out with new products whose names and often rules change what you think you know about a certain kind of investment. One such example of this is annuities. The fixed indexed annuities of today behave nothing like the annuities of yesterday, which is why we'll spend some time clearing up a few myths and misconceptions. This book will walk you through a solid approach to securing income during retirement that includes the following:

- The three-bucket approach: your retirement goals, timeline and what risk tolerance really means.
- Market investments, venture capital and asset protection.
- Common myths about annuities.
- Income planning and pension maximization.
- Getting the most out of Social Security.
- Income creation and laddering strategies.
- Multi-purpose money.
- Taxes and your IRA.
- Legacy planning.

INCOME EXPERTS AND SAFE MONEY SPECIALISTS

We are David and John Compton, co-founders of the independent firm First Security Financial founded in 2000. With our 48 years of cumulative experience, we offer financial services and uncompromising ethics in our mission to help retirees focus on income creation. Over the years as we have worked with hundreds of clients, and we've found that most people DO have enough savings if they take the steps to secure their principal first and maximize all sources of income, including pension benefits, Social Security and the returns on investments generated for income production. Our morning radio shows heard on WRNO 99.5 FM in New Orleans, WJBO 1150 AM in Baton Rouge, KPEL 96.5 FM in Lafayette, and WWL 88.7 AM in New Orleans further educate listeners about safe money strategies and current issues.

With over 50 years of cumulative investment experience, we want you to walk away from reading this book recognizing that you *do* have a way to sustain your retirement income if you take steps now to secure the principal of your investments. If your number one fear is outliving your money, we're here to let you know that there is a way to help make sure this doesn't happen to you. Take care of your principal. Take care of your goose. There may be years when the golden eggs are smaller, but you can survive, thrive and enjoy the retirement you've earned when your income needs are fully secured.

   – David and John Compton, *Founders of First Security Financial; FirstSecurityFinancialShow.com*

1
THE PURPOSE OF
YOUR MONEY

"The seeds of an investment crisis have been sown. The only way to avoid a catastrophe is for plan participants, professionals, and regulators to **shift the mind-set and metrics from asset value to income.**"

— Robert C. Merton

Will your Social Security benefit, 401(k) savings and other retirement assets be enough to support you during retirement? If you're like Lee and Paula, you hope so. When the couple turned 60 years old, they started thinking about what their lives would be like in the next 10 years. When would they retire? What would their retirement look like? How much money did they have? How would they access that money to pay the bills?

9

They could both count on Social Security benefits, but neither one really knew how much their monthly checks would be, or when to file for them. Lee had a modest pension that he could begin collecting at age 67 but he hoped to retire before that time. He also had an IRA worth about $200,000 invested in mutual funds and he wanted to wait until he recaptured his losses from 2008 before moving that money. Paula had a 401(k) valued at $400,000, but she honestly wasn't exactly sure how it worked, how she could draw money from it and how much income it would provide once she retired.

While Lee and Paula may sound like they're totally in the dark about their retirement, the truth is there are a lot of people just like them. They know retirement is coming and know they have some assets to rely on, but they aren't sure how it will all come together to provide them with a retirement income.

You spend your entire working life hoping what you put into your retirement accounts will help you live comfortably once you clock out of the workforce for good. The key word in that sentiment and the word that can make retirement feel like a looming problem instead of a rewarding life stage, is *hope*. You hope you'll have enough money.

Leaving your retirement up to chance is unadvisable by nearly any standard, yet millions of people find themselves hoping instead of planning for a happy ending. With information, tools and professional guidance, creating a successful retirement plan can put you in control of your financial management.

Structuring assets to create an income-generating retirement requires a different approach than earning income via the workforce. Saving money for retirement, which is what you have spent your life doing, and *planning* your retirement are two different things. Both are important. ***Most people spend more time planning their vacations than they spend planning for their retirement.*** While this seems almost unbelievable, the fact is most people only have a vague understanding of what they need to do in order to prepare for retirement. Not knowing what to do or how to plan for it makes it easy to avoid or put off for later. But sometimes later never comes, and many people find themselves applying for their Social Security benefit before they reach the age of maximum payout of their Social Security benefit, exposing their 401(k)s or IRAs to high levels of market risk, and living on a fixed income that doesn't afford them the lifestyle they are accustomed to enjoying.

IDENTIFY YOUR RETIREMENT GOALS AND NEEDS

Today's retirees have redefined what it means to be retired. Answers to the questions, 'what do you want to do during retirement' are as varied as the individual, spanning the gambit from sitting in the easy chair to starting a new company. What are your answers to the question: ***What do you want to do during your retirement?"***

While it seems logical that a retirement plan should begin with questions about money, we like to start by asking questions about you and your life. What are your hopes and dreams? What do you want to do with your time during retirement? Who do you want to do those things with? Who are your family and how often do you see them? Who depends on you? Who do you provide for? Where do you want to live? These questions may sound personal, but money is personal. Money represents more than the paper it's printed on. It is the embodiment of your time, your talents, and your commitments. It buys the food you eat, the house you sleep in, the car you drive, and the clothes you wear. It also helps provide you with the lifestyle you want to live once you retire. If you don't have peace of mind knowing your income is provided for during your retirement years, then what has it all been for?

When the time comes for retirement, you want your money to provide you with a comfortable lifestyle and stable income after your working days are done. You might also have other desires, such as traveling, purchasing property, or moving to be closer to your family (or farther away.) You may also want your assets to provide for your loved ones after you are gone. The truth is that it takes more than just money to fulfill those needs and desires. It takes a comprehensive plan that considers all the working parts of your complicated or not-so-complicated life. That's why we start with questions about you, who you are, and the people close to you. All of this directly impacts your income needs, your plans for retirement, and your future healthcare expenses.

WHAT IS YOUR MONEY FOR?

As the quote at the beginning of this chapter suggests, many retirees lose sight of what their savings are actually for. During your working and earning years as you accumulate and save money, your attention is on the rate of return. Retirement is a time when our focus needs to shift away from the metrics of return rates and onto the ability of an investment to produce income.

When employees have a defined-benefit plan set up for them, and you ask them what their pension is for, they will tell you, "Oh, my pension will replace two-thirds of my income." They look at that pension with the expectation that every month, they'll be getting a check in the mail for X amount of dollars. With today's defined-contribution plans, employees meet with a plan representative to talk about their 401(k), 403(b) or company stock plans NOT in terms of how much income they can produce, but on their ability to generate returns. If you ask them what their 401(k) is doing for them, they will tell you, "Oh, I'm averaging a 17 percent rate of return." The conversation surrounding defined-contribution plans is a conversation about returns, whereas the need for the pension income is still the same. So how do retirees go about converting their saving and investments plans into an income stream they can rely on like a regular pension?

Not all investment products are suitable for producing income, especially in today's low-interest, high market volatility climate. A near-zero percent return on a bank CD may be considered safe in that you can't lose principal, but with outside forces such as inflation and taxes, such a low yield won't sustain your income due to the rapid erosion of your purchasing power. Aggressive market investments and venture capital can also result in catastrophic loss due to volatile market downturns.

The reality is that investment strategies and savings plans that worked in the past have encountered challenging new circumstances that have turned them on their heads. The Great Recession of '08 and '09 highlighted how old investment ideas were not only ineffective but incredibly destructive to the retirement plans of millions of Americans, teaching us that not understanding where your money is invested (and the potential risk o those investments) can work against you. The dawn of an entirely restructured health care system brings with it new options and challenges that will undoubtedly change the way insurance companies provide investment products and services. Saving and investing money isn't enough to truly get the most out of it. You must have a planful approach to managing your assets that refocuses the purpose of your savings away from the return rate and onto what the money was put away for: income.

Identify the purpose of your money. Instead of chasing returns and worrying about how much you can earn, focus on income creation. Think of your 401(k) as your future pension. Leaving that pot of money in the market or using it for an emergency fund means you could find yourself in serious trouble if the market takes another hit like it did in 2008. What worked for your parents or even your parents' parents was probably good advice back then when it came to market investments and venture capital, but people in retirement or approaching retirement today need new ideas and professional guidance. The first step to refocusing your investments begins with identifying how much risk your current investments are exposed to.

WHAT DOES RISK REALLY MEAN?

When the time comes for you to sit down with your financial professional and look at all the investments you currently own, your professional will ask you, "What is your risk tolerance?" Now a lot of people have a lot of different definitions about risk tolerance and what it means, but during your retirement years, it can be boiled down to very simple terms: *How much money do you want to lose?* That's right—your risk tolerance is the money you are comfortable losing. If that money were gone, up in smoke, cooked as a goose, you would be okay with that because you have other resources. It's perfectly okay if your answer to the question, *how much money do you want to lose?*, is none. We don't want you to lose any money either. That's why we talk so ardently about protecting the goose that lays your golden eggs.

Securing income begins with principal protection. We want to take care of the goose—or the principal of your savings—so that she can begin producing the golden eggs of your income. To help clarify the amount of risk your current investments are exposed to, let's take a look at some of the basic truths about money as it relates to saving for retirement.

There are essentially two kinds of money: *Risk Money* and *Safe Money*. Everyone can divide their money into these two categories. Some have more of one kind than the other. The goal isn't to ensure that the funds you are relying on for income are balanced according to your individual needs.

Risk Money is money that is at risk. It fluctuates with the market. It has no minimum guarantee. It is subject to investor activity, stock prices, market trends, buying trends, etc. You get the picture. This money is exposed to more risk but also has the potential for more reward. Because the market is subject to change, you can't really be sure what the value of your investments will be worth in the future. You can't really *rely* on it at all. For this reason, we refer to it as Risk Money. This doesn't mean you should never have any money invested in the market, but it would be dangerous to assume you can know what it will be worth in the future.

Risk Money is an important element of income planning during your accumulation years, when you are working and earning and have time on your side. During those years, you can trade volatility for potential returns, when a longer investment time-frame is available to you. In the long run, time can smooth out the ups and downs of money exposed to the market. Working

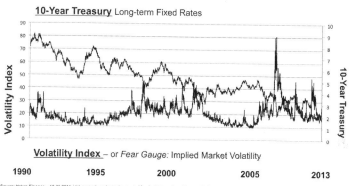

10-Year Treasury Long-term Fixed Rates

Volatility Index – or *Fear Gauge:* Implied Market Volatility

1990　　　　1995　　　　2000　　　　2005　　　　2013

Source: Yahoo Finance · 12-31-2013. VIX is a trademarked ticker symbol for the Chicago Board Options Exchange Market Volatility Index, a popular measure of the implied volatility of S&P 500 index options. Often referred to as the fear index or the fear gauge, it represents one measure of the market's expectation of stock market volatility over the next 30 day period (wikipedia.com) The CBOE 10-year Treasury Note (TNX) is based on 10 times the yield-to-maturity on the most recently auctioned 10-year Treasury note. Past performance does not guarantee future results. Some illustrations may show how a market index has performed. An investor cannot invest in an index, although there are some investments designed to mirror index performance. Past performance is not a guarantee of future results.

The VIX, or volatility index, of the market represents expected market volatility. When the VIX drops, economic experts expect less volatility. When the VIX rises, more volatility is expected.

1. *VIX is a trademarked ticker symbol for the Chicago Board Options Exchange (CBOE) Market Volatility Index, a popular measure of the implied volatility of S&P 500 index options. Often referred to as the fear index or the fear gauge, it represents one measure of the market's expectation of stock market volatility over the next 30 day period. (wikipedia.com)*

2. *The CBOE 10-Year Treasury Note (TNX) is based on 10 times the yield-to-maturity on the most recently auctioned 10-year Treasury note.*

with a professional during your accumulation years to leverage a long-term investment strategy has the potential to create rewarding returns from Risk Money.

Safe Money, on the other hand, is safer when compared to Risk Money. Safe Money is made up of dependable, low-risk or no-risk money, and as such these are investments that you can count on. Social Security is one of the most common forms of Safe Money. Traditional defined-benefit pension plans are also Safe Money. The income you draw or will draw from Social Security and defined-benefit pensions is guaranteed. But how do you turn your defined-contribution plans benefits into Safe Money?

Unlike the market, rates of growth for Safe Money are dependent on 10-year treasury rates. The 10-year treasury, or TNX, is commonly considered to represent a very secure and safe place for your money, hence Safe Money. The 10-year treasury drives key rates for things such as mortgage rates or CD rates. Safe Money may not be as exciting as Risk Money, but it is safer. You can safely be fairly sure you will have it in the future.

Knowing the difference between Risk Money and Safe Money is an important step towards a successful retirement plan. People who are 55 or older and who are looking ahead to retirement should be relying on more Safe Money than Risk Money as they seek to convert their assets into a reliable income stream.

Ideally, the rates of return on Risk Money and Safe Money would have an overlapping area that provided an acceptable rate of risk for both types of money. In the early 1990s, interest rates were high and market volatility was low. At that time, you could invest in either Risk Money or Safe Money options because the rates of return were similar from both investments, and you were likely to be fairly successful with a wide range of options. Today, you don't have those options. Market volatility is at all-time highs while interest rates are at all-time lows. They are so far apart from each other that it is hard to know what to do with your money.

As mentioned earlier, yesterday's investment rules and strategies may not work today. Not only could they hamper achieving your goals, they may actually harm your financial situation. We are currently in a period when the rates for Safe Money options are at historic lows, and the volatility of Risk Money is higher than ever. There is no overlapping acceptable rate, making both options less than ideal. *Because of this uncertain financial landscape, wise investment strategies are more important now than ever.*

This unique situation requires fresh ideas and investment tools that haven't been relied on in the past. Investing the way your parents did will not pay off. The majority of investment ideas used by financial professionals in the 1990s aren't applicable to today's markets. That kind of investing will likely get you in trouble and compromise your retirement. Today, you need a better PLAN.

> » *Michael had a modest brokerage account that he added to when he could. When he changed jobs a couple years ago, at age 62, Michael transferred his 401(k) assets into an IRA. Just a few years from retirement, he is now beginning to realize that nearly every dollar he has saved for retirement is subject to market risk.*
>
> *Intuitively, he knows that the time has come to shift some assets to an alternative that is safer, but how much is the right amount?*

THE RULE OF 100

Another way of shedding light on the amount of risk your assets are currently exposed to is The Rule of 100. This Rule helps shape asset diversification* for the average investor. The rule states that

---

* Asset Diversification disclosure – Diversification and asset allocation does not assure or guarantee better performance and cannot eliminate the risk of investment loss. Before investing, you should carefully read the applicable volatility disclosure for each of the underlying funds, which can be found in the current prospectus.

the number 100 minus an investor's age equals the amount of assets they should have exposed to risk.

> **The Rule of 100**: 100 - (your age) = the percentage of your assets that should be exposed to risk in Risk Money investments.

For example, if you are a 30-year-old investor, the Rule of 100 would indicate that you should be focusing on investing primarily in the market and taking on a substantial amount of risk in your portfolio. The Rule of 100 suggests that 70 percent of your investments should be exposed to risk.

$$100 - (30 \text{ years of age}) = 70 \text{ percent}$$

Now, not every 30-year-old should have exactly 70 percent of their assets in mutual funds and stocks. The Rule of 100 is based on your chronological age, not your "financial age," which could vary based on your investment experience, your aversion or acceptance of risk and other factors.

While it made sense to have 70 percent of your money in the market when you were in your 30s when time was on your side, retirement is a horse of a different color. Risk tolerance generally reduces as you get older. If you are 40 years old and lose 30 percent of your portfolio in a market downturn this year, you have 20 or

30 years to recover it. If you are 68 years old, you have five to 10 years (or less) to make the same recovery. That new circumstance changes your whole retirement perspective. At age 68, it's likely that you simply aren't as interested in suffering through a tough stock market. There is less time to recover from downturns, and the stakes are higher. The money you have saved is money you will soon need to provide you with income, or is money that you already need to meet your income demands.

Ultimately, you are the only person who can answer the question, *what is your risk tolerance*. Everyone has their own level of comfort. Your risk tolerance will be based on your values and attitudes as well as your income goals during retirement. If protecting your principal is important to you during your retirement, then you will want to work with a financial professional who can help you transition your assets away from Risk Money and into Safe Money investments.

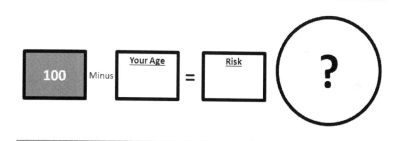

THE THREE-BUCKET PHILOSOPHY

What is your lifestyle today? Would you like to maintain it into retirement? Are there trips you would like to take, or family members you would like to see? Are there any major events such as weddings to pay for down the road that you would like to plan for?

The amount of money you have saved matters, but what you do with that money matters even more. You might have a million dollars socked away in a savings account, but your neighbor who has $300,000 in a structured investment portfolio designed to generate a guaranteed income that supports her lifelong needs may end up enjoying a better retirement lifestyle. Why? Your neighbor had more than a good work ethic and a penchant for saving. They had a planful approach to retirement asset allocation.

Once we've identified your retirement goals and current investment risk, it's time to start taking a look at how we can better position those assets in order to achieve those goals. When making investment choices, always keep in mind what you are using the money for. **The purpose of the money dictates how you position it.** To that end, the Three Bucket system to retirement income planning can be a helpful way to organize your assets. We will be using these same three buckets to for our income creation strategy in a later chapter, but for now, here is a brief introduction to the bucket system and how it works.

Bucket #1 is Your Emergency Fund. During retirement, it is essential that you have an emergency fund you can easily access. Many retirees make the mistake of not having enough money set aside for buying a car, repairing a roof or replacing the windows on the house. The reality is that these things do happen. When the totally unexpected happens, you want a reliable account you can tap into for immediate access to funds. Not having a designated account for large withdrawals can lead to penalties and tax repercussions if you take the money out of tax-qualified accounts or investments designed for the long term.

How much money should you have in Bucket #1? There are exceptions, but ideally, you want to have at least six months and up to one year of emergency money. The most important requirement for the investment vehicles chosen for bucket number one is their function of *liquidity*. You want this money to be liquid so you can access the cash and spend it easily. While it might be frustrating to know that money is sitting there without earning gains, it only takes one unexpected event to make you very glad you planned ahead.

Bucket #2 is The Nest Egg Bucket. Once you have your emergency fund set up, we take the remaining funds and position them to create the most efficient and abundant income streams possible. Your income sources might also include Social Security, a pension or a rental unit that pays you rental income. Strategies for income creation include not just positioning the money into funds, but laddering those funds so you have the opportunities for growth. We will talk more about Need Later money, the laddering strategy and its relationship to liquidity in Chapter Six: Strategies for Income Maximization.

The most important requirement for the investments used for your nest egg is *safety*. The money you are relying on for income must first and foremost be safe. If you lose 50 percent of your nest egg three years after retiring and continue to make withdrawals on that principal, then you have the perfect recipe for outliving your money. Remember the goose in our fable. Securing the nest egg is when you preserve your principal and protect your goose so she can continue delivering the goods.

Bucket #3 is The Risk Bucket. This is where venture capital and market funds come into play. Our philosophy is you can't put money into the third bucket until you have the first two buckets properly filled. Once your emergency fund is in place and your income needs for now and later are met, we can have the conversation about risk tolerance. How much money do you want to lose?

Organizing your assets so they can produce a reliable income stream can quickly become an overwhelming task. The fact of the matter is that financial professionals build their entire careers around understanding the different variables affecting retirement financing. Taking a closer look at your assets might reveal a few surprises and even frustrations, but taking the steps to position those investments so they can secure the income you need will result in a stress-free retirement that you can enjoy.

CHAPTER 1 RECAP //

- Having a planful approach to retirement begins with the individual concerns of you, the investor. What do you want to be doing during your retirement? What are your goals and objectives?

- Most retirees find they are stuck thinking of their investments in terms of the returns they produce rather than in terms of the income they can produce. The purpose of the money dictates how you position it. The purpose of your savings during retirement is to generate income for you.

- The rules for retirement planning have changed. Investing the way your parents did will not pay off and the majority of investment ideas used by financial professionals in the 1990s aren't applicable to today's markets.

- Understanding your risk tolerance is another way of asking yourself, *how much money do you want to lose*? If you don't want to lose any money, then more of your savings should be positioned in Safe Money investments rather than Risk Money investments. With the help of a financial professional, it's easy to see what percentages of your assets are invested in Risk Money investments and what percentage are in Safe Money investments.

- Understanding where and how your assets are invested is key to understanding and securing the safety of your principal. Use the Rule of 100 as a general guiding principle when determining how much risk your retirement investments should be exposed to (100 - [your age] = [percentage of your investments that can comfortably exposed to risk]).

- Using a bucket system can help you achieve your retirement goals. Bucket #1 is an Emergency Fund, Bucket #2 is your Nest Egg, and Bucket #3 is for Risk. The third bucket comes last, after the first two buckets are filled.

2

INVESTMENT MISPERCEPTIONS:
WHAT YOU THINK YOU KNOW

Jack and Emma both retired at the age of 65. Jack had worked hard his whole life, staying with one company and putting away a portion of his paycheck every month into the company 401(k) plan. His wife, Emma, raised their three kids and worked part-time at the local grocery store, but she didn't work enough hours to qualify for benefits. During retirement, they were relying on Jack's substantial savings. He had $550,000 in his 401(k) and for four years, Jack and Emma made regular withdrawals of $2,500 a month to provide for their income needs.

Four years into their retirement, the stock market collapse of 2001 came along and Jack lost roughly 50 percent of his portfolio. For two years he and Emma continued making those $2,500 withdrawals. Watching their account value dwindle, they realized they were in trouble and needed to seek professional help.

By the time Jack and Emma came in to see a financial professional, their $550,000 nest egg had dropped in value to $115,000, and yet they were only six years into their retirement. Jack and Emma were afraid they would run out of money. Jack and Emma were right. According the numbers worked out by their financial professional, if they left their money where it was and continued to make those $2,500 withdrawals, even if the market came back, they would run out of money in four or five years.

Jack and Emma realized they didn't want the stress of not knowing their income was secured. Their financial professional reallocated their remaining $115,000 into an investment product that would pay out $900 of income for them for the rest of their life. This was nowhere near the $2,500 that they needed, however, and so at the age of 70, Jack went back to work pressure cleaning houses.

A lot of people like Jack and Emma make the mistake of entering retirement without first securing the principal of their nest egg. Instead, they do what they have always done and rely on market growth to sustain their savings. They know that what they have done in the past has always worked and so they assume it will continue working for them during retirement. It's easy to see in hindsight where Jack and Emma made their mistake. We tell these stories based on real-life scenarios so that you don't have to make the same mistakes they did.

When the market is good, it's easy to fall under the illusion that a catastrophic loss can't happen to you. It can happen to you. Had Jack and Emma come to their retirement professional with their carefully saved $550,000 nest egg, they would have had more than enough money to provide a stable income for the rest of their lives. Their retirement picture would have included everything they dreamed of: travel, cruises, time with the grandkids, ball games, bowling nights. Instead, the market claimed the lion's share of their hard earned dollars, and they got a very different retirement than they had planned. *More than 90 percent of today's Boomers feel the U.S. is facing a retirement crisis, and more retirees fear outliving their money than they fear even their own death.* * Running out of money doesn't have to be your future if you take the steps now to secure your income needs.

The greatest barriers to retirement planning are the misconceptions that people have about the investments they own and investments products they've heard about. These misconceptions may be stopping you from taking action. This chapter is here to clear up these misconceptions and educate you about what you think you already know.

ARE YOU IN DENIAL ABOUT MARKET RISK?

When it comes to market investments and venture capital, it's not just losing money that matters; **it's when you lose that money.** Investors counsel retirees about a phenomenon known as the Sequence of Returns. You might have some say about your retirement timeline—when you stop working, when you start withdrawing on your savings—but the timeline of the market's performance is at the whims of a global economy.

The years just before and just after retirement are when your savings are at their most vulnerable. Doing the math for the sequence of returns shows us that taking a loss due to stock market fluctuations during those early years can significantly damage your portfolio's ability to sustain you during the long term. The

---

* *http://www.pensionrights.org/publications/fact-sheet/polling-data-americas-retirement-crisis*

sequence of returns dictates that it's not so much the size of the loss, but *when that loss occurs.* Two investors can have the exact same portfolio amounts averaging the same rate of return, but if investor A incurs significant loss ***during the first three years of his retirement,*** followed by gain, he or she will have significantly less money than the investor who incurs the exact same losses during the last three years of retirement.

Timing is everything. Whether the market is high or low at the time of your retirement is out of your control. You do, however, have choices about when you retire, and you can control where your assets are allocated. Don't make the mistake that Jack and Emma did and think that a market correction won't happen to you. Why would you want to leave the security of your retirement up to chance? Why would you want your income roller coastering around at the whims of the market? Why would you want your financial professional to have to tell you, it's time to cut back, you're running out of money? Nobody wants to hear those words. If you secure the principal of your retirement nest egg in a guaranteed investment, you won't have to.

MYTHS ABOUT ANNUITIES

Annuities are one example of an investment product that have gotten such a bad reputations over the years, many people have decided not to have anything to do with them at all. This is a little like throwing out the baby with the bathwater. Don't make the mistake of putting all annuities in the same basket. While it's true that there are annuities out there that aren't suited to income generation, many of today's newer annuities are designed with the current retirement crisis in mind. They offer flexibility, the guarantee of principal protection, and rates of return that are keyed to a market index of your choice. Other features of these newer annuities include bonus money, tax-deferred growth, more money to your beneficiaries and the option of securing an income stream for life without annuitization. If you've been shying away from annuities, then you've been missing out on a large, Safe Money way to both grow your retirement assets and structure them for income.

Chapter Five: Income Creation, goes into all the details about what an annuity is and how they work. The following section is here to shed some light on *what annuities are not* by discussing four myths about this investment that are no longer true.

Myth #1: All Annuities have high fees.

False.

If you have heard rotten things about annuities and high fees, a variable annuity is likely the culprit. These are Risk Money investments sold by licensed brokers or Investment Advisors. While annuities do come from insurance companies, variable annuities are linked to the stock market and the principal balance of a variable annuity is not guaranteed. More to the point, the fees on these annuities can significantly impact your net returns. In addition to income rider fees, variable annuities are connected to multiple mutual funds with a fee attached for the management of each fund. These fees are in addition to the Mortality and Expense fees (listed as M&E fees) and administrative fees. If you add these fees to an income rider or death benefit, the fees on a variable annuity can exceed 4 percent per year.

On the other hand, the fees on most fixed indexed annuities are zero unless you add an income rider, in which case the fee is usually around 1 percent. Annuities without fees do exist, so ask for them.

Myth #2: When you put money in an annuity, you can't access your money.

False.

Many people think that you can't get to your principal with an annuity, but today's indexed income annuities do offer some liquidity. While it's true that most annuities are long term investments, shorter period annuities do exist. Most income annuities today allow you to withdraw up to 10 percent of the account value after the first year without any penalty or surrender charges. That means if you put $100,000 in an annuity offering a 10 percent bonus, and the annuity earns eight percent, after the first year you would have an account balance of $118,800. Should you realize your house needs some significant repairs, you can take out $11,880 from that annuity without being penalized. Income annuities such as the fixed indexed annuity also offer a Minimum Guaranteed Cash Value, also known as a MGCV, which assures you that you will get at least your entire contributed premiums back plus interest when the annuity has matured.

In general, the longer you can set your annuity for growth, the more generous your rate of return will be. You have control over what you decide. Annuities that come with the longest terms of surrender and the highest penalties typically pay the highest rate of interest to your annuity. Shorter terms with smaller penalties exist, and they pay lower rates. In either case, **once an annuity is mature, you can take the lump sum and move it, or do anything else with it you like without any penalty**. You can also renew it and keep it going. With an annuity that's been renewed, there will never be any early withdrawal charges because it is past the surrender charge period.

Myth #3: If you want a guaranteed income for life, you have to give up control of your money.

False.

The reason this myth started is due to one kind of annuity still available today known as *an immediate annuity* with a lifetime income option. If you put your money in an immediate annuity, then it means what its name suggests: the investment starts paying you an income immediately and the principal is said to be *annuitized*. In exchange for this immediate and guaranteed income, you give up access to your principal. Again, this is a choice you get to decide on, because today's retirees have more options when it comes to lifetime income. **Today, you don't have to annuitize an annuity in order to receive a lifetime income option.**

Income annuities such as the fixed indexed annuity can give you a guaranteed lifetime income stream with the purchase of a product known as an income rider. We will go into much greater detail about income annuities in Chapter Five: Income Creation, but for now, it's enough to know that you *can* have control of your money even when it's in an income producing annuity. With income annuities, you have access to the funds and are able to make withdrawals (up to a certain amount) without penalty, and you have the ability to walk away from the investment when the annuity matures if you so desire.

Newer annuities sold after 2009 also offer attractive benefits to your beneficiaries. It used to be that any money left in an annuity reverted back to the insurance company after you died. This is not the case with today's annuities. You now have the option of naming beneficiaries on your annuity so the money you put into the fund goes to the people and causes important to you when you no longer need the income.

Myth #4: Fixed Indexed Annuities offer no opportunity for growth.

False.

A Fixed Indexed Annuity is a specific type of annuity investment product offered by insurance companies that differ from other annuities in that they are linked to the stock market in such a way that allows you to capitalize on the earnings without having to take the hits. Unlike a variable annuity that can fluctuate with the market, a Fixed Indexed Annuity (FIA) **protects** the value of your principal (the full amount that you contribute). FIAs also have built-in safeguards that protect past gains. What you have is a product that offers safety of principal and growth aggressive enough to keep up with inflation.

This specialized type of annuity was once referred to as Equity Indexed Annuities, or EIA. To better understand the unique properties of an indexed investment, it helps to break down the investment according to these terms:

Equity – refers to the amount of money you will put into the annuity. For example, if you have $150,000 saved in a 401(k), and you want to restructure that for a portion of your retirement income, your *equity* would be $150,000.

Indexed – refers to how the annuity is keyed. It may be keyed to the S&P 500 or the Dow Jones Industrial Average or any number of indices. This is how the percentage on your rate of return is calculated. Although keyed to the market, FIAs are considered a Safe Money option because they have a guaranteed principal, meaning you can't lose money in this investment due to market loss.

Annuity – the annual payout of an income.

To specifically address the misconception that FIAs don't offer opportunity for growth, consider a 2003 published study conducted by the nationally recognized Advantage Group. From September 1998 to September 2003, the stock market experienced both incredible growth and incredible loss. Many retirees like Jack and Emma lost huge amounts of money during those years, putting their retirement income at peril. How would their money have done over that same five-year period had it been transferred into an FIA? According to the Advantage Group Research study that examined the performance of the 14 different fixed annuity options available in 1998 (and there are many more available today), fixed indexed annuities that reset annually averaged a return of more than 7 percent per year during that five year span even during the steep market drop experienced in 2001.

Annuities can be a useful investing tool for today's retirees because they are specifically designed to provide a source of income during retirement. You have many choices when it comes to the type of annuity so you want to be aware of the differences between variable, immediate and indexed annuities. A Fixed Indexed Annuity (FIA) purchased with an income rider will pay out a set income without annuitization. Because these annuities are linked to the stock market, they offer opportunity for growth without the volatile up and down swings of the market. There are also no-fee FIAs available. These products can also be used to form an important part of your legacy, providing money for your beneficiaries without the expense and delay of probates.

LONG TERM CARE REALITIES

The common response to the question of long term care is the assumption that it doesn't apply. The misperception that *it won't happen to me* is a very common attitude among today's healthy, independent retirees. As more and more adults find themselves in the position of having to care for an elderly parent, their eyes become opened and their perceptions change. Most people either know someone in a nursing home or are trying to care for a loved on their own. What people are experiencing in their daily lives corresponds to recent statistics that report 70 percent of retirees age 65 will need some form of long term care in their future years, and 20 percent of those cases will require care for five years or longer.*

Still, most people don't see themselves in a nursing home during their retirement, and we can't blame them. Who wants to picture that? **But here's the point we want to make: Planning for long term care isn't about whether or not you will end up in a nursing home. It's about protecting your assets.** It's about saving the goose! The Congressional Budget Office reported in 2004 that seniors in general are not prepared for the costs of long-term care, citing an annual cost of $66,000 for a private room in a nursing home.** Not planning for inevitable issues like health care expenses can devastate your retirement nest egg as drastically as market loss. If these expenses are planned for ahead of time, during the income-planning phase of retirement, you will have a lot more options when it comes to paying for these expenses.

PREPARING FOR THE REALITIES: RISK MONEY AND SAFE MONEY INVESTMENTS

They say what you don't know can't hurt you, but when it comes to retirement planning, that statement simply isn't true. Even if you are unaware of the risk your investments are exposed to, the reality is those risks can still cost you money. There are many factors which can impact the sustainability and longevity of your investments. These factors aren't limited to the realities of long term care and rising health care costs but expand further to include taxes, inflation and the allocation of your assets.

As we've stressed earlier, what you want your money to do for you should dictate your choice of investment vehicles. Proper asset allocation becomes increasingly important as you approach your retirement years. Over the course of your lifetime, it is likely that

---

* *http://longtermcare.gov/the-basics/how-much-care-will-you-need/*
** *http://www.cbo.gov/publication/15584*

you have acquired a variety of assets. Assets can range from money that you have in a savings account or a 401(k), to a pension or an IRA. You have earned money and have made financial decisions based on the best information you had at the time. When viewed as a whole, however, you might not have an overall strategy for the management of your assets. As we have seen, it's more important than ever to know which of your assets are at risk. High market volatility and low treasury rates make for challenging financial topography. Navigating this financial landscape starts with planful asset management that takes into account your specific needs and options.

Knowing the difference between Risk Money and Safe Money is an important step towards a successful retirement plan, yet many investors don't know how much risk they are exposed to. It is helpful to organize your assets so you can have a clear understanding of how much of your money is at risk and how much is in safer holdings. This process starts with listing all your assets. Let's take a look at those assets in relation to the two kinds of money:

To review, Risk Money, as the name indicates, is money that is at risk and may or may not be there when you need it. Risk Money represents what you would like to get out of your investments. Examples of Risk Money include:

- Stock market funds, including index funds
- Mutual funds
- Variable annuities
- REITS

Safe Money is money that you know you can count on. It is safer money that isn't exposed to the level of volatility as the asset types noted above. You can more confidently count on having this money when you need it. Examples of Safe Money are:

- Government backed bonds

- Savings and checking accounts
- Fixed Indexed Annuity (FIA, EIA, or Income Annuities, also sometimes called fixed income annuities.)
- CDs
- Treasuries
- Money market accounts

Safe Money becomes much more important as you age. While you want to reduce the amount of Risk Money you have and to transition it to Safe Money, you don't necessarily need all of it to generate income for you right away. Taking a closer look at Safe Money, you will see there are actually different types. These types are based on when you need the money, which can help you prepare for realties such rising health care costs retirement.

TYPES OF SAFE MONEY:
NEED NOW AND NEED LATER

Money that you need to depend on for income is Safe Money. This Safe Money can be divided into two different pockets depending on when you need this money. There is money used for income now and money used for accumulation to meet your income needs in five, 10 or 20 years. Money needed for income now is Need Now Money. It is money you need to meet your basic needs, to pay your bills, your mortgage if you have one and the costs associated with maintaining your lifestyle. Money used for growth or opportunity is Need Later Money. It's money that you don't need now for income, but will need to rely on down the road. It's still Safe Money because you will rely on it later for income and will need to count on it being there. Need Later Money represents income your assets will need to generate for future use. When planning your retirement, it is vital to decide how much of your assets to structure for income and how much to set aside to accumulate to create Need Later Money.

You must figure out if your income and opportunity needs are met. Your Need Now and Need Later Money are top priorities. Need Now Money, in particular, will dictate what your options for future needs are.

DOES RISK BELONG IN YOUR RETIREMENT?

Experienced investors, people who feel they need to gamble for a higher return, or people who have met their retirement income goals and are looking for additional ways to accumulate wealth are all candidates for investment strategies that incorporate higher levels of risk. In the end, it comes down to your personal tolerance for risk. How much money you willing to lose?

Consulting with a financial professional is often the wisest approach to calculating your risk level. A professional can help determine your risk tolerance by getting to know you, asking you a set of questions and even giving you a survey to determine your comfort level with different types of risk. Here's a typical scenario a financial professional might pose to you:

"You have $100,000 saved that you would like to invest in the market. There is an investment product that could turn your $100,000 into $120,000. That same option, however, has the potential of losing you up to $30,000, leaving you with $70,000."

Is that a scenario that you are willing to enter into? Or are you more comfortable with this one:

"You could turn your $100,000 into $110,000, but have the potential of losing $15,000, leaving you with $85,000."

Your answer to these and others types of questions will help a financial professional determine what level of risk is right for you. Losing money isn't an option you have to accept during your retirement. There are other investment products and strategies available that can help you keep your nest egg intact.

Take a moment to think about your income goals:

Are you happy with your lifestyle? What do you really *need* to live on when you retire? Are there changes that need to be made? Some retirees find that downsizing their home makes sense; others find a move to the country makes sense. Some people will have the luxury of maintaining or improving their lifestyle, while others may have to make decisions about what they need versus what they want during their retirement.

Identifying your retirement goals, organizing your assets, and understanding the amount of risk those assets are exposed to are the basic building blocks of a retirement income plan. Your next step toward income creation is to identify exactly what those income needs are.

CHAPTER 2 RECAP //

- Most people are surprised to find that their investments and assets aren't aligned with their retirement goals. There are many misperceptions out there about investing. Multiple retirement accounts can create confusion about risk. Taking control of your assets begins with determining your exposure to risk.

- The sequence of returns tells us that in addition to how the market performs, the order of those returns is just as important when it comes to calculating the value of our investments.

- There are many myths concerning annuities and what they can and cannot do. Today's annuities can offer you the benefits of market-linked growth and lifetime income without giving up control of your money. Educating yourself about today's annuities can help you make informed choices about investments designed to protect your retirement savings, offer flexibility, opportunity, and guaranteed income.

- Lack of knowledge can cost you retirement dollars in more ways than one. Addressing the realities of long term care and market risk is all about protecting the goose that lays the golden eggs.

- Identify how much of your income you Need Now and how much you Need Later. Once you have your current Need Now income needs supplied, it's crucial to the longevity of your income to plan for Need Later Money. Unexpected expenses such as health care can devastate your nest egg if not planned for carefully.

- Outliving your money is what retirees fear the most. Build your retirement income from a sound foundation of Safe Money.

3

UNDERSTANDING YOUR
INCOME NEEDS

Nancy and Earl sat down with their financial professional to learn about securing their income needs for retirement. Earl was retired and had already started receiving his pension payouts. That pension combined with their Social Security would form the basis for their income. They also had a small amount of savings in an IRA. When the financial professional sat down with them and looked at Earl's paperwork, he realized that the husband took the single payout option on his pension and didn't let his wife know.

"Do you realize," he said to them, "That if anything happens to Earl, Nancy's income during retirement would be cut in half? She wouldn't receive anything at all from your pension."

Nancy and Earl didn't know this. Earl pointed out that he hadn't elected the joint pension option because it would have resulted in

$1,300 less each month, and they needed the money. "I wasn't think-ing about the long term," he confessed. "What can we do to protect Nancy?"

The financial professional helped them secure an income for Nancy using a guaranteed investment tool that would give her MORE income every month than she would have received had Earl elected the joint pension option, and it saved them $300 a month. Jokingly, Nancy turned to her husband and said, "You can go ahead and die now."

Creating an income plan that solves your income needs is about more than just fiddling with a few numbers and arriving at a budget. You must ask the questions: How much money do I need, when do I need it, and who do I need this money for? A lot of couples fail to consider each other's income needs in the singular. As a couple, their combined Social Security benefits, pensions and savings might provide the perfect income, but what happens when one spouse passes away? Answering these questions now will help you make better informed choices about which investment tools to use for the creation of your retirement income.

HOW TO DETERMINE YOUR INCOME NEEDS

Every financial strategy for retirement needs first to accommodate the day-to-day need for income. Finding the most efficient and beneficial way to address your income needs will have impacts on your lifestyle, your asset accumulation and the legacy you leave behind for your loved ones. Take a moment to think about your income goals:

- What is your lifestyle today?
- Would you like to maintain it into retirement?
- Are you meeting your needs?
- Are you happy with your lifestyle?
- What do you really *need* to live on when you retire?

Some people will have the luxury of maintaining or improving their lifestyle, while others may have to make decisions about what they need versus what they want during their retirement. Once you have identified your income need, you will know how much to structure for income now and how much to be set aside for Need Later needs. This is where your Safe Money comes into play: the safer, more reliable assets that you have accumulated that are designed to provide you with a steady income. On day one of your retirement, you will need a steady and reliable supply of income from your Safe Money.

How Much Money Do You Need? While this amount will be different for everyone, the general rule of thumb is that a retiree will require 70 to 80 percent of their pre-retirement income to maintain their lifestyle. Once you know what that number is, the key becomes matching your income need with the correct investment strategies, options and tools to satisfy that need.

When Do You Need Your Money? Will you be retiring next month, in two years? Will you be drawing on a pension or relying soley on your savings and Social Security? Do you plan to liquidate assets such as a home or real estate property? Creating an income plan that lasts as long as you do requires careful planning for 10, 15, and sometimes even 30 years down the road.

If you need your income to last you 10 years, you will want to use a tool that creates just that. If you need a lifetime of income, seek a tool that will do that and without running out. When you take health care costs, potential emergencies, plans for moving or traveling, and other retirement expenses into account, you can really give your calculator a workout. This is why Safe Money becomes much more important as you age.

WHO DO YOU NEED IT FOR?

Poverty after the loss of a spouse is more common among women than men.* Many women find they have fewer options of guaranteed income sources or, like Nancy, they haven't been involved in the decisions about household finances. This often leaves the surviving spouse with 25 to 40 percent less income than what they had been living on.

Spousal continuation is one area where many retirees make grave mistakes (no pun intended.) If your husband or wife is receiving a traditional pension, that income source will disappear when that spouse dies unless you selected a joint option that will provide for the surviving spouse. In some cases, the cost of this joint option is very low—as little as $50 will buy you the peace of mind knowing your spouse is provided for. In other cases, the joint option can cost upwards of a thousand dollars. It might make sense to seek out additional investment tools or products to provide for your spouse rather than relying on your pension options. As in the case of Nancy and Earl above, they saved money AND got a better deal by sitting down with their financial professional and looking at their other options.

Avoiding poverty as a retired widow means taking into considerations what your financial picture would look like if one spouse passes away. There are many investment tools designed to provide spousal continuation, such as life insurance policies that provide for tax-free income and income riders on newer annuity products that offer a joint life option. It's important for both spouses to be involved in the income planning process. If your husband or wife handles all the accounts, make sure you understand how much income will be coming if he or she passes away. Also find out whether or not that income comes from a guaranteed source.

---

* *http://www.ssa.gov/policy/docs/ssb/v65n3/v65n3p31.html*

WHERE IS THIS MONEY COMING FROM?
INCOME THAT CAN'T BE CHANGED

The first place we look for income producing sources are Safe Money options such as pensions and Social Security. The amount of income provided by those sources can't be changed, and they provide the retirement base that you build up from until you reach the number you need. A financial professional can help you customize an income plan based on your retirement goals and current expenses by utilizing a strategy that provides for both growth and opportunity to meet your Need Now and Need Later income requirements.

CHAPTER 3 RECAP //

- The foundation of a retirement strategy depends on knowing how much money you need, when you need it and who you need it to provide for.

- Spousal continuation is one area often overlooked by retirees. When one spouse dies, the loss of pensions and monetary benefits such as Social Security means a reduction in monthly income. Your income plan should take into consideration guaranteed sources of income that will still be available after your spouse passes away.

- Some annuities offer joint life options with the purchase of an income rider. These income riders continue to supply a monthly income even after one spouse passes away as opposed to single income riders.

4

MAXIMIZING SOCIAL SECURITY

One kind of Green Money that most Americans rely on for income when they retire is Social Security. If you're like most Americans, Social Security is or will be an important part of your retirement income and one that you should know how to properly manage. As a first step in creating your income plan, a financial professional will take a look at your Social Security benefit options. Social Security is the foundation of income planning for anyone who is about to retire and is a reliable source of Green Money in your overall income plan.

> » *Mary had worked full-time nearly her entire adult life and was looking forward to enjoying retirement with her husband, kids and grandkids. When she turned 62, she decided*

to take advantage of her Social Security benefits as soon as they became available.

A couple of years later, she was organizing some of the paperwork in her home office. She came across an old Social Security statement, and remembered the feeling of filing and beginning a new phase in her life.

However, as she looked over the statement, she realized in retrospect that she might have been better off waiting to file for benefits. She had saved enough to wait for benefits, and if she had, her monthly benefit could have been quite a bit more.

When she was in the process of retiring, there were so many other decisions to make. It seemed very straightforward to file right away. She made a note to call the Social Security Administration to see if it was possible to change her monthly benefit to the larger amount.

Here are some facts that illustrate how Americans currently use Social Security:

- Nearly 90 percent of Americans age 65 and older receive Social Security benefits.*
- Social Security provides about 39 percent of the income of the elderly.*
- Claiming Social Security benefits at the wrong time can reduce your monthly benefit by up to 65 percent.**
- In 2013, 36 percent of men and 40 percent of women claimed Social Security benefits at age 62.***

---

* https://www.ssa.gov/pressoffice/basicfact.html

** https://www.ssa.gov/planners/retire/retirechart.html

*** Trends in Social Security Claiming, Alicia H Munnell and Anqi Chen, Center for Retirement Research, May 2015. http://crr.bc.edu/wp-content/uploads/2015/05/ IB_15-8.pdf

- In 2013, more than a third of workers claimed Social Security benefits as soon they became eligible.*
- In 2015, the average monthly Social Security benefit was $1,328. The maximum benefit for 2015 was $2,663. The $1,335 monthly benefit reduction between the average and the maximum is applied for life.*

There are many aspects of Social Security that are well known and others that aren't. When it comes time for you to cash in on your Social Security benefit, you will have many options and choices. Social Security is a massive government program that manages retirement benefits for millions of people. Experts spend their entire careers understanding and analyzing it. Luckily, you don't have to understand all of the intricacies of Social Security to maximize its advantages. You simply need to know the best way to manage your Social Security benefit.

You need to know exactly what to do to get the most from your Social Security benefit and when to do it. Taking the time to create a roadmap for your Social Security strategy will help ensure that you are able to exact your maximum benefit and efficiently coordinate it with the rest of your retirement plan.

There are many aspects of Social Security that you have no control over. You don't control how much you put into it, and you don't control what it's invested in or how the government manages it. However, you do control when and how you file for benefits. The real question about Social Security that you need to answer is, "When should I start taking Social Security?" While this is the all-important question, there are a couple of key pieces of information you need to track down first.

Before we get into a few calculations and strategies that can make all the difference, let's start by covering the basic informa-

---

* *https://www.ssa.gov/news/press/factsheets/colafacts2015.html*

tion about Social Security which should give you an idea of where you stand. Just as the foundation of a house creates the stable platform for the rest of the framework to rest upon, your Social Security benefit is an important part of your overall retirement plan. The purpose of the information that follows is not to give an exhaustive explanation of how Social Security works, but to give you some tools and questions to start understanding how Social Security affects your retirement and how you can prepare for it.

Let's start with eligibility.

Eligibility. Understanding how and when you are eligible for Social Security benefits will help clarify what to expect when the time comes to claim them.

To receive retirement benefits from Social Security, you must earn eligibility. In almost all cases, Americans born after 1929 must earn 40 quarters of credit to be eligible to draw their Social Security retirement benefit. In 2015, a Social Security credit represents $1,220 earned in a calendar quarter. The number changes as it is indexed each year, but not drastically. In 2014, a credit represented $1,200. Four quarters of credit is the maximum number that can be earned each year. In 2015, an American would have had to earn at least $4,880 to accumulate four credits. In order to qualify for retirement benefits, you must have earned a minimum number of credits.

Additionally, if you are at least 62 years old and have been married to a recipient of Social Security benefits for at least 12 months, you can choose to receive Spousal Benefits. Although 40 is the minimum number of credits required to begin drawing benefits, it is important to know that once you claim your Social Security benefit, there is no going back. Although there may be cost of living adjustments made, you are locked into that base benefit amount forever.

Primary Insurance Amount. You can think of your Primary Insurance Amount (PIA) like a ripening fruit. It represents the amount of your Social Security benefit at your Full Retirement Age (FRA). Your benefit becomes fully ripe at your FRA, and will neither reduce nor increase due to early or delayed retirement options. If you opt to take benefits before your FRA, however, your monthly benefit will be less than your PIA. You will essentially be picking an unripened fruit. On the one hand, waiting until after your FRA to access your benefits will increase your benefit beyond your PIA. On the other hand, you don't want the fruit to overripen, because every month you wait is one less check you get from the government.

Full Retirement Age. Your FRA is an important figure for anyone who is planning to rely on Social Security benefits in their retirement. Depending on when you were born, there is a specific age at which you will attain FRA. Your FRA is dictated by your year of birth and is the age at which you can begin receiving your full monthly benefit. Your FRA is important because it is half of the equation used to calculate your Social Security benefit. The other half of the equation is based on when you start taking benefits.

When Social Security was initially set up, the FRA was age 65, and it still is for people born before 1938. But as time has passed, the age for receiving full retirement benefits has increased. If you were born between 1938 and 1960, your full retirement age is somewhere on a sliding scale between 65 and 67. Anyone born in 1960 or later will now have to wait until age 67 for full benefits. Increasing the FRA has helped the government reduce the cost of the Social Security program, which paid out almost $870 billion to beneficiaries in 2015!*

While you can begin collecting benefits as early as age 62, the amount you receive as a monthly benefit will be less than it would be if you wait until you reach or surpass your FRA. It is important

---

* *https://www.ssa.gov/news/press/basicfact.html*

to note that if you file for your Social Security benefit before your FRA, *the reduction to your monthly benefit will remain in place for the rest of your life.* You can also delay receiving benefits up to age 70, in which case your benefits will be higher than your PIA for the rest of your life.

- At FRA, 100 percent of PIA is available as a monthly benefit.
- At age 62, your Social Security retirement benefits are available. For each month you take benefits prior to your FRA, however, the monthly amount of your benefit is reduced. This reduction stays in place for the rest of your life.
- At age 70, your monthly benefit reaches its maximum. After you turn age 70, your monthly benefit will no longer increase.

Year of Birth	Full Retirement Age
1943-1954	66
1955	66 and 2 months
1956	66 and 4 months
1957	66 and 6 months
1958	66 and 8 months
1959	66 and 10 months
1960 or later	age 67*

ROLLING UP YOUR SOCIAL SECURITY

Your Social Security income "rolls up" the longer you wait to claim it. Your monthly benefit will continue to increase until you turn 70 years old. Even though Social Security is the foundation of most people's retirement, many Americans feel that they don't

* *http://www.ssa.gov/OACT/progdata/nra.html*

have control over how or when they receive their benefits. The truth is that every dollar you increase your Social Security income by means less money you will have to spend from your nest egg to meet your retirement income needs, but many retirees do not take advantage of this fact. For many people, creating their Social Security strategy is the most important decision they can make to positively impact their retirement. *The difference between the best and worst Social Security decision can be tens of thousands of dollars over a lifetime of benefits.*

Deciding NOW or LATER: Following the above logic, it makes

YEAR OF BIRTH	FULL RETIREMENT AGE
1943-1954	66
1955	66 and 2 months
1956	66 and 4 months
1957	66 and 6 months
1958	66 and 8 months
1959	66 and 10 months
1960 or later	67*

sense to wait as long as you can to begin receiving your Social Security benefit. However, the answer isn't always that simple. Not everyone has the option of waiting. Many people need to rely on Social Security on day one of their retirement. Some might need the income. Others might be in poor health and don't feel they will live long enough to make waiting until their FRA worthwhile for themselves or their families. It is also possible, however, that the majority of folks taking an early benefit at age 62 are simply under-informed about Social Security. Perhaps they make this major decision based on rumors and emotion.

---

http://www.ssa.gov/OACT/progdata/nra.html

File Immediately if You:
- Find your job is unbearable.
- Are willing to sacrifice retirement income.
- Are not healthy and need a reliable source of income.

Consider Delaying Your Benefit if You:
- Want to maximize your retirement income.
- Want to increase retirement benefits for your spouse.
- Are still working and like it.
- Are healthy and willing / able to wait to file.

So if you decide to wait, how long should you wait? Lots of people can put it off for a few years, but not everyone can wait until they are 70 years old. Your individual circumstances may be able to help you determine when you should begin taking Social Security. If you do the math, you will quickly see that between ages 62 and 70, there are 96 months in which you can file for your Social Security benefit.

If you take into account those 96 months and the 96 months your spouse could also file for Social Security, and the number of different strategies for structuring your benefit, you can easily end up with more than 20,000 different scenarios. It's safe to say this isn't the kind of math that most people can easily handle. Each month would result in a different benefit amount. The longer you wait, the higher your monthly benefit amount becomes. Each month you wait, however, is one less month that you receive a Social Security check.

The goal is to maximize your lifetime benefits. That may not always mean waiting until you can get the largest monthly payment. Taking the bigger picture into account, you want to find out how to get the most money out of Social Security over the number of years that you draw from it. Don't underestimate the power of optimizing your benefit: the difference between the BEST and WORST Social Security election can easily be worth thousands of dollars in lifetime benefits. **The difference can be very substantial!**

If you know that every month you wait, your Social Security benefit goes up a little bit, and you also know that every month you wait, you receive one less benefit check, how do you determine where the sweet spot is that maximizes your benefits over your lifetime? Financial professionals have access to software that will calculate the best year and month for you to file for benefits based on your default life expectancy. You can further customize that information by estimating your life expectancy based on your health, habits and family history. If you can then create an income plan (we'll get into this later in the chapter) that helps you wait until the target date for you to file for Social Security, you can optimize your retirement income strategy to get the most out of your Social Security benefit. How can you calculate your life expectancy? Well, you don't know exactly how long you'll live, but you have a better idea than the government does. They rely on averages to make their calculations. *You have much more personal information about your health, lifestyle and family history than they do.* You can use that knowledge to game the system and beat all the other people who are making uninformed decisions by filing early for Social Security.

While you can and should educate yourself about how Social Security works, the reality is you don't need to know a lot of general information about Social Security in order to make choices about your retirement. What you do need to know is exactly *what to do to maximize your benefit.* Because knowing what you need to do has huge impacts on your retirement! For most Americans, Social Security is the foundation of income planning for retirement. Social Security benefits represent about 39 percent of the income of the elderly.* For many people, it can represent the largest portion of their retirement income. Not treating your Social Security benefit as an asset and investment tool can lead to sub-optimization of your largest source of retirement income.

Let's take a look at an example that shows the impact of working with a financial professional to optimize Social Security benefits:

> » George and Mary Bailey are a typical American couple who have worked their whole lives and saved when they could. George is 60 years old, and Mary is 56 years old. They sat down with a financial professional who logged onto the Social Security website to look up their PIAs. George's PIA is $1,900 and Mary's is $900.
>
> If the Baileys cash in at age 62 and begin taking retirement benefits from Social Security, they will receive an estimated $568,600 in lifetime benefits. That may seem like a lot, but if you divide that amount over 20 years, it averages out to around $28,400 per year. The Baileys are accustomed to a more significant annual income than that. To make up the difference, they will have to rely on alternative retirement income options. They will basically have to depend on a bigger nest egg to provide them with the income they need.
>
> If they wait until their FRA, they will increase their lifetime benefits to an estimated $609,000. This option allows them to achieve their Primary Insurance Amount, which will provide them a $34,200 annual income.
>
> After learning the Baileys' needs and using software to calculate the most optimal time to begin drawing benefits, the Baileys' financial professional determined that the best option for them drastically increases their potential lifetime benefits to $649,000!

* https://www.ssa.gov/OACT/progdata/nra.html

> *By using strategies that their financial professional recommended, they increased their potential lifetime benefits by as much as $80,000. There's no telling how much you could miss out on from your Social Security if you don't take time to create a strategy that calculates your maximum benefit. For the Baileys, the value of maximizing their benefits was the difference between night and day. While this may seem like a special case, it isn't uncommon to find benefit increases of this magnitude. You'll never know unless you take a look at your own options.*

Despite the importance of knowing when and how to take your Social Security benefit, many of today's retirees and pre-retirees may know little about the mechanics of Social Security and how they can maximize their benefit.

So, to whom should you turn for advice when making this complex decision? Before you pick up the phone and call Uncle Sam, you should know that the Social Security Administration (SSA) representatives are actually prohibited from giving you election advice! Plus, SSA representatives in general are trained to focus on monthly benefit amounts, not the lifetime income for a family.

MAXIMIZING YOUR LIFETIME BENEFIT

As discussed earlier, calculating how to maximize lifetime benefits is more important than waiting until age 70 for your maximum monthly benefit amount. It's about getting the most income during your lifetime. Professional benefit maximization software can target the year and month that it is most beneficial for you to file based on your life expectancy.

The three most common ages that people associate with retirement benefits are 62 (Earliest Eligible Age), 66 (Full Retirement Age), and 70 (age at which monthly maximum benefit is reached).

In almost all circumstances, however, none of those three most common ages will give you the maximum lifetime benefit.

Remember, every month you wait to file, the amount of your benefit check goes up, but you also get one less check. You don't know how exactly how long you're going to live, but you have a better idea of your life expectancy than the actuaries at the Social Security Administration who can only work with averages. They can't make calculations based on your specific situation. A professional can run the numbers for you and get the target date that maximizes your potential lifetime benefits. You can't get this information from the SSA, but you can get it from a financial professional.

Types of Social Security Benefits:
- Retired Worker Benefit. This is the benefit with which most people are familiar. The Retired Worker Benefit is what most people are talking about when they refer to Social Security. It is your benefit based on your earnings and the amount that you have paid into the system over the span of your career.
- Spousal Benefit. This is available to the spouse of someone who is eligible for Retired Worker Benefits.
- Survivorship Benefit. When one spouse passes away, the survivor is able to receive the larger of the two benefit amounts.
- Restricted Application. A higher-earning spouse may be able to start collecting a spousal benefit on the lower-earning spouse's benefit while allowing his or her benefit to continue to grow. Due to the Bipartisan Budget Act of 2015, this option is only available to individuals who turned age 62 before January 1, 2016.

In November of 2015, the Bipartisan Budget Act of 2015 was passed, which will have a dramatic impact on the way many Americans plan for Social Security. As the largest change to Social

Security since 2000, the Bipartisan Budget Act of 2015 eliminated an estimated $9.5 billion* of benefits to retirees and may limit some of the flexibility you previously had to structure your benefits.

In 2000, Congress passed the Senior Citizens Freedom to Work Act. The bill allowed retirees to suspend receiving benefits so they wouldn't be subject to additional taxation if they chose to return to work after they filed for Social Security. However, by doing so, the bill also unintentionally created several loopholes in claiming strategies: most notably, the Restricted Application for spousal benefits and "file and suspend" filing strategy. For most Americans, the Bipartisan Budget Act of 2015 closed these loopholes by eliminating "file and suspend" and the Restricted Application.

The new rules mandate that:
- If a primary worker is not currently receiving benefits, then their dependents (child, spouse) can no longer collect benefits based on the primary worker's earning record.
- If you file for benefits, then you are filing for all benefits to which you are entitled – not just the benefit type you choose.

It's important to remember that in spite of these immense changes, one thing stayed the same – filing for Social Security is one of the most important financial decisions you will make in your lifetime, and a financial professional can help ensure you make the right one.

THE DIVORCE FACTOR

How does a divorced spouse qualify for benefits? If you have gone through a divorce, it might affect the retirement benefit to which you are entitled.

---

* *https://www.ssa.gov/OACT/progdata/nra.html*

In general, a person can receive benefits as a divorced spouse on a former spouse's Social Security record so long as the following conditions are met:

- the marriage lasted at least 10 years; and
- the person filing for divorce benefits is at least age 62, unmarried, and not entitled to a higher Social Security benefit on his or her own record.*

With all of the different options, strategies and benefits to choose from, you can see why filing for Social Security is more complicated than just mailing in the paperwork. Gathering the data and making yourself aware of all your different options isn't enough to know exactly what to do, however.

On the one hand, you can knock yourself out trying to figure out which options are best for you and wondering if you made the best decision. On the other hand, you can work with a financial professional who uses customized software that takes all the variables of your specific situation into account and calculates your best option.

You have tens of thousands of different options for filing for your Social Security benefit. If your spouse is a different age than you are, it nearly doubles the amount of options you have. This is far more complicated arithmetic than most people can do on their own.

If you want a truly accurate understanding of when and how to file, you need someone who will ask you the right questions about your situation, someone who has access to specialized software that can crunch the numbers. The reality is that you need to work with a professional that can provide you with the sophisticated analysis of your situation that will help you make a truly informed decision.

---

* http://www.ssa.gov/retire2/yourdivspouse.htm

Important Questions about Your Social Security Benefit:

- How can I maximize my lifetime benefit? By knowing when and how to file for Social Security. This usually means waiting until you have at least reached your Full Retirement Age. A professional has the experience and the tools to help determine when and how you can maximize your lifetime benefits.
- Who will provide reliable advice for making these decisions? Only a professional has the tools and experience to provide you reliable advice.
- Will the Social Security Administration provide me with the advice? The Social Security Administration cannot provide you with advice or strategies for claiming your benefit. They can give you information about your monthly benefit, but that's it. They also don't have the tools to tell you what your specific best option is. They can accurately answer how the system works, but they can't advise you on what decision to make as to how and when to file for benefits.

The Maximization Report that your financial professional will generate represents an invaluable resource for understanding how and when to file for your Social Security benefit. When you get your customized Social Security Maximization Report, you will not only know all the options available to you – but you will understand the financial implications of each choice.

In addition to the analysis, you will also get a report that shows exactly at what age – including which month and year – you should trigger benefits and how you should apply. It also includes a variety of other time-specific recommendations, such as when to apply for Medicare or take Required Minimum Distributions from your qualified plans. A report means there is no need to wonder, or to try to figure out when to take action – the Social

Security Maximization Report lays it all out for you in plain English.

CHAPTER 4 RECAP //

- To get the most out of your Social Security benefit, you need to file at the right time.
- A financial professional can help you determine when you should file for Social Security to get your Maximum Lifetime Benefit.

5

INCOME CREATION:
SAFETY AND OPPORTUNITY WITH THE SAME DOLLAR

After assessing your income needs and maximizing your Social Security, you will then calculate the difference between the guaranteed sources of income you have and the income you need. If your monthly Social Security check and your other supplemental income leave a shortfall, this is called the **Income Gap.** The retirement savings you have so carefully managed over the years is what most retirees rely on in order to fill this income gap. The money you have tucked away into your company 401(k) or IRA is now going to be restructured to provide you with enough income to support you during retirement. The job of efficiently turning those savings into an income stream that can't be outlived is a mighty one. You want to choose investment tools and products that can accomplish the three important objectives of *safety, growth and income*.

As we introduced earlier, the safety of your income producing investment is paramount. This harkens back to the Aesop fable, the Goose that Laid the Golden Egg. If you don't take care of the goose, there will be no more golden eggs. The goose in this scenario represent the principal of your retirement savings, and now is when you are going to determine where to put the goose. Where will she be the most protected and the most likely to thrive?

Ideally, you want to seek an investment vehicle that can guarantee the base of your principal. That means regardless of what the market does, the goose stays intact. That being said, you also want your goose to be well-fed, with opportunities to stretch her wings. Is there an investment vehicle out there that can provide both principal protection and growth? Can you get both safety and opportunity with the same dollar? You can, and that investment tool is called an income annuity.

THE CURRENT SCOOP ON ANNUITIES

Indexed annuities have been around since 1995 and annuities in general date back to the Roman times. If you have developed a bad opinion about annuities, ask yourself, when did you first develop your perception of annuities? Was it 15 years ago? Thirty years ago? When you purchased a fixed annuity at a bank? When you heard about a friend who had a variable annuity with high fees? What experience did you have that gave you the base of your fundamental understanding about annuities?

We covered many common assumptions about annuities that are no longer true earlier in Chapter Two: Investment Misperceptions. It's true there are many different kinds of annuities, and not all of them are suitable for creating income during retirement. Not only are there different kinds of income annuities, but when it comes to indexed annuities, there are also different ways to calculate the gains. How those gains are calculated can make a big difference on the kinds of returns you see when seeking growth within your annuity. This chapter delves deeper into the inner working of annuities and how they work. Income annuities can be broken down to two types: those that require annuitization and those that do not.

THE TWO ANNUITIES: WHAT YOU NEED TO KNOW TO PROTECT YOUR MONEY

While there are many different kinds of annuities with add-on benefits and features, when it comes to their ability to payout a lifetime stream of income, you can simplify things by breaking them down into two categories: those that require annuitization and those that don't.

To annuitize means to convert a lump sum amount of money into an income stream. When you annuitize, you give up control of your principal in exchange for an income stream. There are some annuities today that still operate this way using annuitization, but there are a good many annuities that DON'T require annuitization in order to supply an income stream. What this means is that you can still have control of your money even while it's producing the income.

One type of income annuity sold today that still requires annuitization is known as the SPIA, or Single Premium Immediate Annuity. As the name suggests, you would choose an SPIA if your income needs were immediate. A Single Premium Immediate Annuity is simply a contract between you and an insurance company that allows you to convert a lump sum of money into an income you can start drawing on next month for an agreed upon time period. That time period could be five years, or it could be for the remainder of your lifetime.

SPIAs provide investors with an immediate stream of reliable income when they can't afford to take the risk of losing money in a fluctuating market. One downside to a SPIA is that you are locked into whatever the interest rate is at the time you purchase the contract. While this interest rate is guaranteed to never drop, it will never go up, either. If today's interest rate gives you enough opportunity to meet your income needs, and you do not need access to the principal, then a SPIA is one way to reduce your risk while giving you regular payments that begin right after you buy the contract.

Oftentimes, people make the mistake of simply choosing the highest lifetime benefit when purchasing an SPIA, but this option may not provide you with the guarantees that you need to protect your spouse or beneficiaries. Make sure to ask your financial professional about your options for putting a guarantee on the contract. Guarantees from insurance companies are based on the claims-paying ability of the issuing insurance company.

A Fixed Indexed Annuity (FIA) with an income rider offers a way to generate a guaranteed income stream for life without annuitization. With FIAs, you still have control of your principal while receiving the income payouts. We will go into more detail about the internal workings of these products, but the key to how these annuities are able to generate sustainable returns has to do with a feature known as indexing. This feature allows the investment to track any one of a number of investment indexes chosen by the investor. The indexed annuity is linked to the market without being directly invested in the market, so your goose is protected from the wolves of stock market thievery. What's more, you are also given the guarantee that you won't lose any principal from market corrections. For the retiree worried about running out of money, this can be your ticket to peace of mind.

There are other annuities sold with income riders such as the variable annuity that **do not** give retirees the same guarantees of principal, so watch out for these. In summary:

Single Premium Immediate Annuities (SPIAs) offer guarantee of principal and an income for life payout, but they do require annuitization.

Fixed Indexed Annuities (FIAs) offer guarantee of principal, market linked growth and the option of income for life payout without annuitization.

Variable Annuities (VA) do NOT offer guarantee of principal and are considered a Risk Money investment. They offer participation in market growth (and loss) and the option of income for life payout but taking the income payout means losing control of the principal. Variable annuities also have high fees.

The following example shows just how helpful an indexed annuity option can be for a retiree:

> » Dan and Carol are 62 years old and have decided to run the numbers to see what their retirement is going to look like. They know they currently need $6,000 per month to pay their bills and maintain their current lifestyle. They have also done their Social Security homework and have determined that, between the two of them, they will receive $4,200 per month in benefits. They also receive $350 per month in rent from a tenant who lives in a small carriage house in their backyard. Between their Social Security and the monthly rent income, they will be short $1,450 per month.
>
> They do have an additional asset, however. They have been contributing for years to an IRA that has reached a value of $350,000. They realize that they have to figure out how to turn the $350,000 in their IRA into $1,450 per month for the rest of their life.
>
> At first glance, it may seem like they will have plenty of money. With some quick calculations, they find they have 240 months, or nearly 20 years, of monthly income before they exhaust the account. When you consider income tax, the

potential for higher taxes in the future, and market fluctuations (because many IRAs are invested in the market), the amount in the IRA seems to have a little less clout. Every dollar Dan and Carol take out of the IRA is subject to income tax, and if they leave the remainder in the IRA, they run the risk of losing money in a volatile market. Once they retire and stop getting a paycheck every two weeks, they also stop contributing to their IRA. And when they aren't supplementing its growth with their own money, they are entirely dependent on market growth. That's a scary prospect. They could also withdraw the money from the IRA and put it in a savings account or CD, but removing all the money at once will put them in a tax bracket that will claim a huge portion of the value of the IRA. A seemingly straightforward asset has now become a complicated equation! Dan and Carol didn't know what to do, so they met with their financial professional.

Their financial professional suggested that they use the money to purchase an indexed annuity with an income rider. They selected an annuity that was designed for their specific situation. They took the lump sum from their IRA, placed it in an indexed annuity taking advantage of annual reset so they never lost the value of their investment. In return, they were guaranteed the $1,450 of income per month that they needed to meet their retirement goals. The simplicity of the contract allowed them to do an analysis with their professional just once to understand the product. They basically put their money in an investment crockpot where they didn't have to look at it or manage it. They just needed to let it simmer. In fact, their professional was able to find an annuity for them that allowed them their $1,450 monthly payment with a lump sum of $249,455, leaving them more than $100,000 to reinvest somewhere else. Keep in mind that annuities are *tax deferred, meaning you will pay tax on the income you receive from an annuity in the year you receive it.*

How much income your investments must provide depends on the size of your income gap and when you need the income. If retirement is in your future, it may be possible to do a reverse calculation by starting with the income you need and your timeline. If you have a one to five year window, for example, you might be able to increase your contributions or let your money roll up or grow in an income annuity in preparation for those future withdrawals.

HOW TO WIN THE GAME

When a couple like Dan and Carol come in to talk about retirement planning before their account drops due to market loss, we tell them, *Congratulations, you have won the game.* They have enough money saved to enjoy a comfortable retirement, to travel, to do the things they have always dreamed of doing. All they have to do is protect their nest egg, reallocate their investments for income production and turn on the income stream when ready. This is good news and exactly what we like to see.

When structuring an investment for income production, it's important to base your calculation on the value of the guaranteed returns as opposed to the hypothetical return. The **hypothetical** rate of return is a projection based on the current rate. If the current rate is good, then this hypothetical scenario will no doubt look very appetizing. The **guaranteed** rate of return is the real rate and the number that the insurance company can guarantee. It's important to realize that a lot of agents and representatives base their numbers on a hypothetical projection because that will cast their product in the best light. Remember, the purpose of this investment is to create income, not returns. You want to make sure that when it comes to the performance of the investment, the worst-case scenario will give you what you need. If you get more than what you need, great! This will give you a track to run on based on the worst possible numbers and not pie-in-the-sky numbers.

There are also situations where people come in and they don't need to turn their retirement savings into an income stream. They have enough money coming in through other guaranteed sources, and so their use of an income annuity is a little different. They might elect to put their savings in an indexed annuity with an income rider because of the opportunity these products can provide. They aren't trying to protect themselves from the worst-case scenario, but rather they want to capitalize on the best-case scenario of growth and safety using the same investment dollar. Indexed annuities can be purchased with a death rider benefit that guarantees their beneficiaries will receive the remainder of the account balance at the time of their death. This provides an opportunity to create legacy money and secure growth without chasing around returns.

In summary, income annuities are an investment that can provide you with a reliable source of income for the rest of your life much like Social Security, but you get to control how much money you put in and when you take it out. It also has the potential to increase the value of your principal investment and provide a substantial legacy for your loved ones.

It's not about whether the market goes up or down, but when it does. If it goes down at the wrong time for your five or 10 year retirement horizon, you could be in serious danger of losing principal and retirement income, thus cooking your goose. If you have assets that you would like to structure for retirement income, *an income annuity may be the right choice for you.*

HOW ANNUITIES FIT INTO AN OVERALL INCOME PLAN

In its simplest form, an annuity is a way to invest your money that allows you to structure it for income. Annuities come in a variety of modes. Finding the right one for you will take a conversation with your financial professional. Be sure you fully understand the features, benefits and costs of any annuity you are considering before investing money.

Here is how an income annuity can work:

When you put your money into an annuity, you are essentially buying an investment product from an insurance company. It is a contract between you and the insurance company that provides the investment tool. Let's say you have saved $100,000 and need it to generate income to meet your needs above and beyond your Social Security and pension checks. You give the $100,000 to an insurance company, who in turn invests it to generate growth.

The insurance company will usually select investments that have modest returns over long term horizons. In other words, they generally put it somewhere stable and predictable. Most commonly, they will invest it in a combination of bonds and treasuries that are safer and dependable ways to grow money. They use the money from the insurance products they sell to invest, use a portion of the returns to generate profits for themselves, and return a portion to clients in the form of payouts, claims, and structured income options.

One of the most attractive qualities of these types of annuities is something called annual reset. Annual reset is sometimes also referred to as a "ratcheting." Instead of taking on the risk that comes with putting money in a fluctuating market, you can protect your principal and gains from market volatility. It works like this: If the market goes down, you don't suffer a loss. But if the market goes up, you get percentage of the gains locked in.

The amount of gain you get is called your annuity participation rate. Typically the insurer will cap the amount of gain you can realize at somewhere between 3 and 7 percent. If the market goes up 10 percent, you would realize a portion of that gain (whatever percentage you are capped at). This means you to never lose money on your investment, while always gaining a portion of the upswings. The measurement period of your annuity can be calculated monthly, weekly and even daily, but most annuities are measured annually. The level of the index when you buy and the index level one year later will determine the amount of loss or gain. You and the insurance company are betting that the market will generally go up over time.

Here is how your rates are determined:

To calculate the growth rate, your insurance company can use what's known as a point-to-point annual system or the point-to-point monthly. With the annual system, the calculations are done once a year or every two to five years, depending on the annuity. Indexed annuities receive their credited growth because they are keyed to an index such as the S&P 500 or the Dow Jones Industrial Average or any number of indexes. Although keyed to the market, all annuities except for variable annuities are considered a Safe Money option because they have a guaranteed principal, meaning you can't lose principal due to market loss. How much you gain depends on how the rates are capped.

Here is a brief summary of how the caps for income riders on indexed annuities can work:

Point to point annual – On the day that your money goes into the annuity, the insurance company will take a reading on the keyed index and note what the index is at on that day. On the one year anniversary of your annuity, they will take the reading again. Is the difference between the two readings a plus, or is it a minus?

If it is a minus, nothing happens, because you can't suffer a loss with a fixed indexed income annuity. If the difference is a plus, the percentage is calculated using the caps set forth by the terms of the contract. For example, let's say your cap is at 4.5 percent. Even if the gain for that year was 7 percent, your annuity only earns 4.5 percent. If the gain was 2 percent, your annuity earns 2 percent.

Point to point monthly – Instead of reading the index at the end of one year, the reading is done on a monthly basis. This means there will be a total of 12 readings. For example, let's say you have a monthly point-to-point strategy with a 1.7 percent cap. From January to February, the index goes up by 1 percent, so you get a 1 percent gain. Next month, the index goes up again and you receive a 1.5 percent gain. In the third month, the index goes down 3 percent which will net a negative, but this negative is only used to calculate the rate, it does not mean that your account balance will go down. In the fourth month, the index saw a 3 percent gain, but your cap is at 1.7, so you receive a 1.7 gain.

To calculate your rate of return, you add all the positive gains and subtract the negatives. During a consistent rise in the market, you can see some very nice rising returns on an indexed annuity using point-to-point monthly. Remember, even though the negative gains are used to calculate your rate of return, your account value on indexed annuities cannot lose any money due to loss, so if the average is a negative, the worst thing that could happen is your would earn zero percent for the year.

WHAT IS AN INCOME RIDER?

One desirable optional feature with indexed annuities is the additional purchase of an income rider. Income riders are designed to provide safety of principal and a guaranteed lifetime income to people who are worried about running out of money during retirement. Here is how they work:

When you use that $100,000 to buy a contract with an insurance company in the form of an annuity, you are pegging your money on an index. It could be the S&P 500, the Dow Jones Industrial Average or any number of indexes. Because of the power of annual reset, you are able to retain the gains earned from the index of your choice when it goes up, without losing principal when the index goes down.

To generate income from the annuity, you select something called an income rider. An income rider is a feature or add-on benefit like upgrading your hotel suite or flying business first class, so you do pay an extra percentage for this feature. In return, you get more opportunity for your dollar. Essentially, the income rider creates a separate account which shows a different rate of growth from which the insurance company will pay you an income. When you receive your statements from the annuity, you will notice two different account names and account values.

Income Value: Your income value is a larger number than what your investment is actually worth, and if you select the income rider, it will increase in value over time, providing you with more income.

For example, if you have an income value growing at 6.5 percent and in in 6 years' time you need the income, the amount of your income stream is based on the amount in the income value account.

This value cannot be taken in a lump sum nor is it passed on to your heirs, but it is used to determine your guaranteed lifetime income payout.

Indexed Value: Your actual money and the money you DO have access to is still in the account value growing according to the indexing terms set forth in the contract. The indexed value will go down as your income is paid out, but it will also be replenished by the returns. If this account ever reaches zero, you would still continue to receive your monthly income payments because those payments are guaranteed by the income rider. As the insurance company holds your money and invests it, they generate a return on it that they use to pay you a regular monthly income based on the higher number of either the Indexed Value or the Income Value created by the income rider. Upon death, the Index Value is used to determine what is paid out to heirs. If the annuity matures at the end of the contract, this is the lump sum that you can walk with.

Remember, insurance companies make long-term investments that provide them with predictable flows of money. They like to stabilize the amount of money that goes in and out of their doors instead of paying and receiving large unpredictable chunks at once. When you opt for an income rider, an insurance company

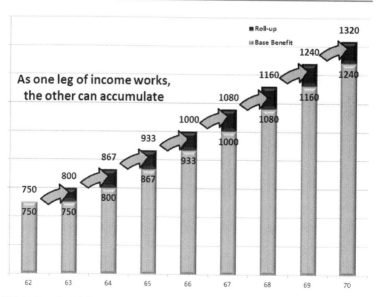

This is a hypothetical illustration

can reliably predict how much money they will pay out to you over a set period of time. It's predictable, and they like that. They can base their business on those predictable numbers.

HOW TO MAINTAIN CONTROL OVER YOUR MONEY

In order to encourage investors to leave their money in their annuity contracts, insurance companies create surrender periods that protect their investments. It is important that most companies offer you 10 percent free access to you money per year with no penalties. However, if you take more than 10 percent it will be subject to a surrender charge. A typical surrender period is 10 years. If after three years you decide that you want your $100,000 back, the insurance company has that money tied up in bonds and other investments with the understanding that they will have it for another seven years. Because they will take a hit on removing the money from their investments prematurely, you will have to pay a surrender charge that makes up for their loss. During the surrender period, an annuity is not a demand deposit account like a savings or checking account. The higher returns that you are guaranteed from an annuity are dependent on the timeframe you selected. The longer an insurance company can hold your money, the easier it is for them to guarantee a predictable return on it.

If you leave your money in the annuity contract, you get a reliable monthly income no matter what happens in the market. **Once the surrender period has expired, you can remove your money whenever you want.** Your money becomes liquid again because the insurance company has used it in an investment that fit the timeline of your surrender period. For many people, this is an attractive trade off that can provide a creative solution for filling their income gap.

When is an annuity with an income rider right for you? A good financial professional can help you make that determination by taking the time to listen closely to your situation and understanding what your needs are as you enter retirement. Every salesperson has a bag full of brochures and PowerPoint presentations, but they need to know exactly what the financial concerns of their individual clients are in order to help them make the most informed and beneficial decision. Some people need income today, others need it in five or 10 years. Others may have their income needs met but are planning to move closer to their children and will need to buy a house in 10 years. Or, if you want income in 15 years, you might want to choose a different investment product for 10 years, and then switch to an annuity with an income rider during the last five years of your timeline. Everyone's situation is different and everyone's needs are different. People who are interested in annuities, however, usually need to make decisions that affect their income needs, whether it is filling their income gap, or providing for income down the road.

VARIABLE ANNUITIES: FOUR QUESTIONS YOU NEED TO ASK

As mentioned earlier, variable annuities can lose money with market fluctuations. As their name suggests, they vary with the market. These annuities *do not* take advantage of annual reset when the market goes down. The income value from the income rider will stay the same, but the value of your actual contract (the indexed value) may fall. If you surrender the annuity, the insurance company will pay you the market value of the asset, regardless of whether it matches, exceeds or falls short of the value at which you bought the contract. If its value has dropped significantly, you may be better off taking the income rider without surrendering your contract.

Variable annuities are sometimes sold by professionals who don't fully understand the product themselves, so it's important to know what questions to ask in order to protect yourself. The following four questions are designed to help you determine whether or not a variable annuity is in your best interest.

Question #1: Does my variable annuity require annuitization? Some of the newer variable annuities coming out today do not require annuitization with the purchase of an income rider.

Question #2: Does my variable annuity have a joint payout for my spouse? Find out whether or not it matters whose name is on the annuity.

Question #3: What are the fees? You might want to specifically ask about all the fees, charges and costs associated with your variable annuity. Sometimes variable annuity costs hide in the corners under names such as M&E expenses or administration charges.

Question #4: What is my market risk? A variable annuity does provide opportunity and can give you income, but you have to temper this with the market risk and high fees. It is a Risk Money investment and not a Safe Money investment.

Just like any investment strategy, the amount of risk needs to fit the comfort level of the investor. Annuities are no exception. Be sure you understand the features, benefits, costs and fees associated with any annuity product before you invest.

CREATING AN INCOME

Creating an income plan before you retire allows you to satisfy your need for lifetime income and ensures that your lifestyle can last as long as you do. You also want to create a plan that operates in the most efficient way possible. Doing so will give more security to your Need Later Money and will potentially allow you to build your legacy down the road. There are many strategies you can use to maximize the income streams from your annuity. One strategy using the three bucket approach involves multiple income creation products as shown in the following story:

» *Diane is 60 years old and is wondering how she can use her assets to provide her with a retirement income. She will be retiring in six years and has $450,000 in an IRA account, $150,000 in after tax money, and a 401(k) account valued at $250,000. If she starts withdrawing her Social Security benefit at age 66, it will provide her with $2,200 per month. Diane calculates her income needs and finds that she will require another $1,480 to meet her goals; however that number may increase down the road. Diane wants to know how she can give herself a pay raise if needed to cover any increase in her expensses.*

According to the rules of a typical brokerage account, Diane should withdraw 4 percent from a $500,000 account, but relying on this strategy exposes the majority of her assets to risk. Diane wants her income to be safe and guaranteed.

Working with a financial professional and using a laddering strategy, Diane is actually able to generate more income using less money. She organizes her assets into three buckets of money: one bucket for emergency funds, one bucket for her nest egg money that will generate income, and a third bucket for venture capital.

With the help of her financial professional, Diane puts her $150,000 into a savings account for emergency expenses in her bucket number one. To fill her income gap, she positions $250,000 from her IRA into a fixed indexed annuity with a 7 percent income rider roll up rate. In six years, this will generate $19,461.00 annually to provide her with $1621.75 a month in income for the rest of her life. This will take care of her projected income gap, but what if she needs more money?

In a second laddered account, Diane places $100,000 into an annuity with a 6.5 percent income rider roll up rate. In 12 years, that investment will generate $12,763.00 annually, or another $1063.00 a month of income for the rest *of her life. Laddered in a third account she places $100,000 in another indexed annuity with an income rider left to grow for 18 years. With a 6.5 percent roll up rate, this investment will generate another lifetime income stream of $20,674.78 or $1,723.00 a month for life.*

Diane's financial professional positions the accounts so that every six years, Diane can give herself a pay raise if needed using her IRA dollars. If she doesn't need the money, she doesn't have to take the income. She also keeps her $250,000 in bucket number three for venture capital and still contributes to her 401(k).

The total of all the laddered accounts is $450,000, and this is able satisfy all her current and future income needs with no risk to her principal. She is able to accomplish this using less money than normally required for a typical brokerage account.

Using annuities for income generation includes the following steps:

- Review your income needs and look specifically at the shortfall you may have during each year of your retirement based on your Social Security income, and income from any other assets you have.
- Ask yourself where you are in your payout or income phase. Is retirement one year away? 10 years away? Last year?
- Determine how much money you need and how you need to structure your existing assets to provide for that need.
- If you have an asset from which you need to generate income, consider options offered by purchasing an income rider on an annuity.

CHAPTER 5 RECAP //

- After Social Security and your additional income is accounted for, the amount that's left to meet your needs is called the *Income Gap*. An income annuity such as a fixed index annuity is one financial tool designed with the specific needs of today's retirees in mind.

- Income producing annuities can be broken down into two categories: those that require annuitization and those that do not. A Single Premium Immediate Annuity has the ability to give you an immediate, lifetime income, but requires annuitization. A Fixed Indexed Annuity purchased with an income rider can also give you lifetime income without annuitization.

- To annuitize means to give up control of the lump sum of your principal in exchange for a guaranteed income stream. Today's new annuities can give you a guaranteed lifetime income without annuitization. Annuities with income riders give you both guaranteed income and control of your principal. The income can go up in value as you wait to trigger a monthly check.

- •Although an indexed annuity is an income-producing asset that does not subject your income to market risk, it still has the opportunity to grow. Indexed annuities participate in market growth without market loss through an indexing strategy. This combined with the power of annual reset gives you both growth and the guaranteed safety of your principal.

- •The benefits of an indexed income annuity include: guarantee of principal, a minimum guaranteed cash value, no fees, access to your money, bonus money, tax deferral, and a guaranteed lifetime income.

- Be sure you understand the features, benefits, costs and fees associated with any annuity product before you invest.

6
STRATEGIES FOR INCOME MAXIMIZATION

"Moving to an income-focused pension strategy will require changes not only to the way retirement plan providers actually invest the money but also to how they engage and communicate with savers."
— Robert C. Merton

Art was a 52-year electrician who had saved $1 million in his company 401(k) plan working for Bell South. In looking over his investment returns, Art realized that all of his savings were in company stock with no options for preserving that money. He was so worried about losing everything he had worked and saved for, Art gave up his job and reallocated the funds. He invested his $1 million in venture capital and market funds, in what he thought was a more balanced portfolio.

Right before the '08 market plunge, his broker called him and advised that he pull out his money and go to all cash. Art was alarmed, but did as the broker suggested. He was stunned when he realized the loss he had narrowly escaped. Two months later, Art came in to see a financial professional about retirement planning.

After hearing his story, the financial planner asked him, "Why are you here? Your broker did right by you. He was one of the few that was paying attention and you didn't lose any money."

"Yes," Art replied, "I'm here because my broker isn't in the business of income. You are."

Throughout the book, we have discussed how today, investment options requires advice that is relevant to today. Traditional, outdated investment strategies are not only ineffective; they can be harmful to the average investor. One of the most traditional ways of thinking about investing is the risk versus reward trade-off. It goes something like this:

Investment options that are considered safer carry less risk, but also offer the potential for less return. Riskier investment options carry the burden of volatility and a greater potential for loss, but they also offer a greater potential for large rewards. Most professionals move their clients back and forth along this range, shifting between investments that are safer and investments that are structured for growth. Essentially, the old rules of investing dictate that you can either choose relative safety *or* return, but you can't have both.

Updated investment strategies work with the flexibility of liquidity to remake the rules. Here is how:

There are three dimensions that are inherent in any investment: *Liquidity, Safety,* and *Return.* You can maximize any two of these dimensions at the expense of the third. If you choose Safety and Liquidity, this is like keeping your assets in a checking account or savings account. This option delivers a lot of Safety and

Liquidity, but at the expense of any Return. On the other hand, if you choose Liquidity and Return, meaning you have the potential for great return and can still reclaim your money whenever you choose, you will likely be exposed to a very high level of risk. One strategy we employ for the maximization of income creation is a three bucket philosophy that allows for a balanced approach to safety, liquidity and return.

THE THREE BUCKET STRATEGY

This solution to the liquidity/safety/return dilemma is an important part of income planning because people are living longer now than they used to. Maximizing your dollars will help them to stretch further into the future to address long term care needs, rising taxes and inflation. One strategy for the maximization of your money is the structuring of three separate accounts, organized with your short and long term objectives in mind. This is the bucket strategy we covered in Chapter Two. Here is a breakdown of investments suitable for this strategy and how they relate to liquidity, safety and return.

Bucket #1 Your Emergency Fund: The two components required for investments in bucket one are *liquidity* and *safety*. You want to be able to access this money quickly and easily should an unexpected expense pop up such as car repairs or an unplanned trip. The money is placed in a checking account, savings, or money market account. Choosing a mutual fund for your emergency money gives you liquidity at the expense of safety, but this liquidity is not as it appears. Should the mutual fund account drop by 50 percent, you've essentially rendered the account non-liquid, because most people will want to recoup their losses. This means waiting for the market to come back before accessing the money, and who knows how long this wait could be. Meeting regularly with your financial professional will ensure that the account is replenished as needed.

Bucket #2 The Nest Egg Bucket: The two components required for investments in your nest egg bucket are *safety* and *growth*. This is money designed for your income needs both now and later. You want this money to be in Safe Money investments with a guaranteed principal because you are relying on the funds to pay the bills for both the short and long term. You also need this money to be earning some rate of return so you don't lose purchasing power to inflation. Suitable investment vehicles for bucket two include a mix of indexed annuities laddered for the long term. Laddering is a strategy whereby multiple investments are purchased and set for different time periods. This allows you to capitalize on the best interest rates while structuring income for 5, 10 and 20 years down the road. Choosing a more aggressive investment that doesn't provide for protection of your principal is one way retirees risk running out of money. Taking a market hit during the first three years of their retirement can devastate an income plan, which is why *safety* is the most important element of income producing investments.

Bucket #3 The Risk Bucket: The two components of the risk bucket are *growth* and *liquidity*. After properly funding buckets one and two, you have the option of placing the addition funds in riskier investments. Have a conversation with your financial professional about risk tolerance. The opportunity for growth might not be worth the trade-off of the risk, depending on what you want to use the money for. Remember, the purpose of the money dictates how you position it.

Taking control of your assets and protecting your principal is where the muscle of your plan really goes to work for you. As you set your strategy into motion, it's important to revisit the plan at least annually. Your financial professional should stay in touch with you to make adjustments, re-strategize, and fine-tune your plan as life events such as weddings, births, divorce, and new cars come into play. When these life-events crop up, it's important to pull the needed funds from the right bucket in order to avoid costly mistakes to your retirement assets.

UNDERSTANDING THE TRADE-OFF

Understanding Liquidity can help you break the old Risk versus Safety trade-off. By identifying assets from which you don't require Liquidity, you can place yourself in a position to potentially profit from relatively safe investments that provide a higher than average rate of return. Choosing Safety and Growth over Liquidity can have significant impacts on the growth opportunity available to your assets. In the following example story of Sawyer and his liquid investment portfolio, the paradigm shift from earning and saving to leveraging assets was a costly one.

> » *Sawyer is a corn and soybean farmer with 1,200 acres of land. He routinely retains somewhere between $40,000 and $80,000 in his checking and savings accounts. If a major piece of equipment fails and needs repair or replacement, Sawyer will need the money available to pay for the equipment and carry on with farming. If the price of feed for his cattle goes up one year, he will need to compensate for the increased overhead to his farming operation. He isn't a particularly wealthy farmer, but he has little choice but to keep a portion of money on hand in case something comes up and he must access it quickly. Most of his capital is held in livestock in the pasture or crops in the ground tied up for six to eight months of the year. When a major financial need arises, Sawyer can't just harvest 10 acres of soybeans and use*

them for payment. He needs to depend heavily on Liquidity in order to be a successful farmer.

Old habits die hard, however, and when Sawyer finally hangs up his overalls and quits farming, he keeps his bank accounts flush with cash, just like in the old days. After selling the farm and the equipment, Sawyer keeps a huge portion of the profits in Liquid investments because that's what he is familiar with. Unfortunately for Sawyer, with his pile of money sitting in his checking account, he isn't even keeping pace with inflation. After all his hard work as a farmer, his money is losing value every day because he didn't shift to a paradigm of leveraging his assets to generate income and accumulate value.

Almost anything would be a better option for Sawyer than clinging to Liquidity. He could have done something better to get either more return from his money or more safety, and at the very least would not have lost out to inflation.

As yourself, how much Liquidity do you *really* need?

Think about it. If you haven't sat down and created an income strategy for your retirement, your perceived need for Liquidity is a guess. You don't know how much cash you'll need to fill the income gap if you don't know the amount of your Social Security benefit or the total of your other income options. If you *have* determined your income need and have made a plan for filling your income gap, you can partition your assets based on when you will need them. With an income plan in place, *you can use new rules to enjoy both Safety and Return from your assets.*

CHAPTER 6 RECAP //

- The three aspects of any investment include liquidity, safety, and growth. You can choose to maximize any two against the third.

- A three-bucket approach to your money can provide liquidity when you need it, with safety and growth for the security of your retirement income. This will help ensure that your money lasts as long as you do.

- A comprehensive income plan during retirement should include provisions for an emergency fund. This fund should be a liquid account you can readily access.

- Choosing to maximize liquidity alone can be an expensive option because the sooner you need your money back, the less you can leverage it for safety and growth. To plan for a successful retirement in today's economy requires a creative use of today's financial tools.

7
HOW TO COOK A GOOSE
THE STOCK MARKET AND YOUR SAVINGS

Everyone has different goals and plans in during retirement, but everyone also needs income. Your retirement savings is the asset you are relying on to supply you with that income. Time and time again history has shown us that not protecting the principal of your savings and exposing it to market risk during retirement results in such a significant loss to the investment principal, many retirees never recover. Going back to our goose analogy, these retirees end up like the hapless couple in the fairy tale, with no goose and no golden eggs. Once your goose is cooked due to market loss and your principal is cut in half, the chances of outliving your money increase. To learn more about how to cook your goose, read on.

RECIPEE FOR DISASTER

It can be challenging to watch the stock market's erratic changes every month, week or even every day. When you have your money riding on it, the ride can feel pretty bumpy. When you are managing your money by yourself, emotions inevitably enter into the mix. The Dow Jones Industrial Average and the S&P 500 represent more to you than market fluctuations. They represent your retirement goals. It's hard not to be emotional about it.

Everyone knows you should buy low and sell high. But this is what is more likely to happen:

The market takes a downturn, similar to the 2008 crash, and investors see as much as a 30 percent loss in their stock holdings. It's hard to watch, and it's harder to bear the pain of losing that much money. The sequence of returns means that if they retire in the years directly before or after the loss, their funds have a much greater chance of dwindling quickly, with no chance of recuperation. So they sell and hope to preserve what's left. But eventually, and inevitably, the market begins to rise again. Maybe slowly, maybe with some moderate growth, but by the time the average investor notices an upward trend and wants to buy in again, they have already missed a great deal of the gains.

> » *Virginia worked for a paper mill company for 34 years. During her time there, she acquired bonuses and pay raises that often included shares of stock in the company. She also dedicated part of her paycheck every month to a 401(k) that bought stock in the company. By the time she retired, Virginia has $250,000 worth of company stock.*
>
> *Although she had contributed to her 401(k) account every month, Virginia didn't cultivate any other assets that*

could generate income for her during retirement. Virginia also retired early at age 62 because of her failing health. The commute to work every day was becoming difficult in her weakened condition and she wanted to enjoy the rest of her life in retirement instead of working in the cramped office of the paper mill company.

Because she retired early, Virginia failed to maximize her Social Security benefit. While she lives a modest lifestyle, her income needs are $3,500 per month. Virginia's monthly Social Security check only covers $1,900, leaving her with a $1,600 income gap. To supplement her Social Security check, Virginia sells $1,600 of company stock each month to meet her income needs. A $250,000 401(k) is nothing to sneeze at, but reducing its value by $1,600 every month will decimate her savings within 10 years. And that's if the market stays neutral or grows modestly. If the market takes a downturn, the money that Virginia relies on to fill her income gap will rapidly diminish. Even if the market starts going up in a couple of years, it will take much larger gains for her to recover the value that she lost due to the math of rebounds (which will be explained shortly).

Unhappily for Virginia, she retired in 2007, just before the major market downturn that lasted for several years. She lost more than 20 percent of the value of her stock. Because Virginia needed to sell her stock to meet her basic income needs, the market price of the stock was secondary to her need for the money. When she needed money, she was forced to sell however many shares she needed to fill her income gap that month. And if she has a financial crisis, involving a need for long term medical care, for example, she will be forced to sell stock even if the market is low and her shares are nearly worthless.

*Virginia realizes that she could have relied on an invest-
ment structured to deliver her a regular income while protecting the value of her investment. She could have kept her
$250,000 from diminishing while enjoying her lifestyle into
retirement regardless of the volatility of the market. Ideally,
Virginia would have restructured her 401(k) to reflect the
level of risk that she was able to take. In her case, she would
have had most of her money in a Safe Money assets, allowing
her to rely on the value of her assets when she needed them.*

EMOTIONS AND MONEY

In 2013, DALBAR, the well-respected financial services market
research firm, released their annual "Quantitative Analysis of
Investment Behavior" report (QAIB). The report studied the
impact of market volatility on individual investors: people like
Lisa, or anyone who was managing (or mismanaging) their own
investments in the stock market.

According to the study, volatility not only caused investors
to make decisions based on their emotions, those decisions also
harmed their investments and prevented them from realizing
potential gains. So why do people meddle so much with their
investments when the market is fluctuating? Part of the reason
is that many people have financial obligations that they don't
have control over. Significant expenses like house payments, the
unexpected cost of replacing a broken-down car, and medical bills
can put people in a position where they need money. If they need
to sell investments to come up with that money, they don't have
the luxury of selling when they *want* to. They must sell when they
need to.

DALBAR's "Quantitative Analysis of Investor Behavior" has
been used to measure the effects of investors' buying, selling and
mutual fund switching decisions since 1994. The QAIB shows
time and time again over nearly a 20 year period that the average

investor earns less, and in many cases, significantly less than the performance of mutual funds suggests. QAIB's goal is to improve independent investor performance and to help financial professionals provide helpful advice and investment strategies that address the concerns and behaviors of the average investor.

An excerpt from the report claims that:

"QAIB offers guidance on how and where investor behaviors can be improved. No matter what the state of the mutual fund industry, boom or bust: Investment results are more dependent on investor behavior than on fund performance. Mutual fund investors who hold on to their investments are more successful than those who time the market.

QAIB uses data from the Investment Company Institute (ICI), Standard & Poor's and Barclays Capital Index Products to compare mutual fund investor returns to an appropriate set of benchmarks.

There are actually three primary causes for the chronic shortfall for both equity and fixed income investors:

1. *Capital not available to invest. This accounts for 25 percent to 35 percent of the shortfall.*
2. *Capital needed for other purposes. This accounts for 35 percent to 45 percent of the shortfall.*
3. *Psychological factors. These account for 45 percent to 55 percent of the shortfall."*

The key findings of Dalbar's QAIB report provide compelling statistics about how individual investment strategies produced negative outcomes for the majority of investors:

- Psychological factors account for 45 percent to 55 percent of the chronic investment return shortfall for both equity and fixed income investors.

- Asset allocation is designed to handle the investment decision-making for the investor, which can materially reduce the shortfall due to psychological factors.
- Successful asset allocation investing requires investors to act on two critical imperatives:
    1. Balance capital preservation and appreciation so that they are aligned with the investor's objective.
    2. Select a qualified allocator.
- The best way for an investor to determine their risk tolerance is to utilize a risk tolerance assessment. However, these assessments must be accessible and usable.
- Evaluating allocator quality requires analysis of the allocator's underlying investments, decision making process and whether or not past efforts have produced successful outcomes.
- Choosing a top allocator makes a significant difference in the investment results one will achieve.
- Mutual fund retention rates suggest that the average investor has not remained invested for long enough periods to derive the potential benefits of the investment markets.
- Retention rates for asset allocation funds exceed those of equity and fixed income funds by over a year.
- Investors' ability to correctly time the market is highly dependent on the direction of the market. Investors generally guess right more often in up markets. However, in 2012 investors guessed right only 42 percent of the time during a bull market.
- Analysis of investor fund flows compared to market performance further supports the argument that investors are unsuccessful at timing the market. Market upswings rarely coincide with mutual fund inflows while market downturns do not coincide with mutual fund outflows.

- Average equity mutual fund investors gained 15.56 percent compared to a gain of 15.98 percent that just holding the S&P 500 produced.
- The shortfall in the long-term annualized return of the average mutual fund equity investor and the S&P 500 continued to decrease in 2012.
- The fixed-income investor experienced a return of 4.68 percent compared to an advance of 4.21 percent on the Barclays Aggregate Bond Index.
- The average fixed income investor has failed to keep up with inflation in nine out of the last 14 years.*

It doesn't take a financial services market research report to tell you that market volatility is out of your control. The report does prove, however, that before you experience market volatility, you should have an investment plan, and when the market is fluctuating, you should stand by your investment plan. You should also review and discuss your investment plan with your financial professional on a regular basis, ensuring he/she is aware of any changes in your goals, financial circumstances, your health or your risk tolerance. When the economy is under stress and the markets are volatile, investors can feel vulnerable. That vulnerability causes people to tinker with their portfolios in an attempt to outsmart the market. Financial professionals, however, don't try to time the market for their clients. They try to tap into the gains that can be realized by committing to long-term investment strategies.

THE TIMING OF THINGS

We mentioned the sequence of returns earlier in Chapter Two, but it bears mentioning again here. Time is the one crucial ingredient necessary for aggressive accumulation that retirees in particular

---

2013 QAIB, Dalbar, March 2013

don't have a lot of. Losing a chunk of the savings you are relying on for income means you don't have the *time* to make those gains back because you need the money to live on now. For example, if you are a retiree with $100,000 in market investments, and a market correction like the one we saw in 2008 comes along, your account balance can drop by as much as 50 percent. So now you only have $50,000. While it may be true that the market always comes back, how long will it take *you* to make that $50,000 back? How will you achieve that while making those withdrawals to pay the bills? More importantly, what does that $50,000 mean to you now? Do you have to rethink your retirement plans? Will you have to go back to work? During retirement, most people don't have the luxury of waiting another 10 years while the market comes back.

The sequence of returns is another factor that impact retirees in particular. Whether the market is high or low at the time of your retirement is out of your control, yet it influences your account value even more than the actual rate of return. Let's take a look at the following example:

> » *Walter and Sue retired in 1995. They had $500,000 invested in venture capital and are taking out $25,000 per year to fill their income gap and achieve their desired retirement income. The value of their account at the end of the year 2013 was $1,200,000.*
>
> *Their neighbors, Matthew and Betty Jo, are a few years younger, and they retired in the year 2000. They did exactly the same thing as Walter and Sue, withdrawing $25,000 per year from a $500,000 investment held in the stock market. The value of their account at the end of the year 2013 was $94,000.*

This difference in the size of their savings is due to the sequence of returns. The only thing Matthew and Betty Jo did differently was to retire five years later, yet that played a huge role in how their gains were calculated. During the first three years of their retirement, they took three big hits during the market corrections of 2001 when Enron collapsed, the WorldCom collapse of 2002, and the market fall of 2003 when Martha Stewart was indicted. During Walter and Sue's retirement, those same three big hits were calculated at the end of the 13-year period as opposed to at the beginning.

You have no control over world events, the behavior of politicians, CEOs or celebrities. Do you want your retirement to be based on things you have no control over? You do have control over the allocation of your assets. You can make the choice to keep the goose of your principal safe and secured, so she can continue laying the golden eggs of your income for years to come.

CHAPTER 7 RECAP //

- To cook a goose, take one large retirement savings account, put it in the stock market, wait for a downturn, and watch the money burn away.
- The timing of market downturns is more critical to retirees than to the average investor. If you are making withdrawals on a market investment without principal guarantees, and the account suffers a loss, rapid depletion of your funds will change what the future of your retirement looks like.
- The sequence of returns tells us that in addition to how the market performs, the order of those returns is just as important when it comes to calculating the value of your account.
- Emotions inevitably enter the mix during stock market downturns. According to the DALBAR "Quantitative Analysis of Investment Behavior" report released in 2013, the average fixed income investor managing their money alone failed to keep up with inflation in nine out of the last 14 years.

8

TAXES AND
RETIREMENT

Everyone is familiar with taxes (you've been paying them your entire working life), but not everyone is familiar with how to make tax planning a part of their retirement strategy.

Tax planning and *tax reporting* are two very different things. Most people only *report* their taxes. March rolls around, people pull out their 1040s or use TurboTax to enter their income and taxable assets, and ship it off to Uncle Sam at the IRS. If you use a CPA to report your taxes, you are essentially paying them to record history. You have the option of being proactive with your taxes and to plan for your future by making smart, informed decisions about how taxes affect your overall financial plan. Working with a financial professional who, along with a CPA, makes recommendations about your finances to you, will keep you looking forward instead of in the rearview mirror as you enter retirement.

PAYING LESS TAX DURING YOUR RETIREMENT

When you retire, you move from the earning and accumulation phase of your life into the asset distribution phase of your life. For most people, that means relying on Social Security, a 401(k), an IRA, or a pension. Wherever you have put your Safe Money for retirement, you are going to start relying on it to provide you with the income that once came as a paycheck. Most of these distributions will be considered income by the IRS and will be taxed as such. There are exceptions to that (not all of your Social Security income is taxed, and income from Roth IRAs is not taxed), but for the most part, your distributions will be subject to income taxes.

Regarding assets that you have in an IRA or a 401(k) plan that uses an IRA, when you reach 70 ½ years of age, you will be required to draw a certain amount of money from your IRA as income each year. That amount depends on your age and the balance in your IRA. The amount that you are required to withdraw as income is called a Required Minimum Distribution (RMD). Why are you required to withdraw money from your own account? Chances are the money in that account has grown over time, and the government wants to collect taxes on that growth. If you have a large balance in an IRA, there's a chance your RMD could increase your income significantly enough to put you into a higher tax bracket, subjecting you to a higher tax rate.

Here's where tax planning can really begin to work strongly in your favor. In the distribution phase of your life, you have a predictable income based on your RMDs, your Social Security benefit and any other income-generating assets you may have. What really impacts you at this stage is how much of that money you keep in your pocket after taxes. Essentially, *you will make more money saving on taxes than you will by making more money.* If you can reduce your tax burden by 30, 20 or even 10 percent, you earn yourself that much more money by not paying it in taxes.

How do you save money on taxes? By having a plan. In this instance, a financial professional can work with the CPAs at their firm to create a **distribution plan** that minimizes your taxes and maximizes your annual net income.

BUILDING A TAX DIVERSIFIED PORTFOLIO

So far so good: avoid taxes, maximize your net annual income and have a plan for doing it. When people decide to leverage the experience and resources of a financial professional, they may not be thinking of how distribution planning and tax planning will benefit their portfolios. Often more exciting prospects like planning income annuities, investing in the market and structuring investments for growth rule the day. Taxes, however, play a crucial role in retirement planning. Achieving those tax goals requires knowledge of options, foresight and professional guidance.

Finding the path to a good tax plan isn't always a simple task. Every tax return you file is different from the one before it because things constantly change. Your expenses change. Planned or unplanned purchases occur. Health care costs, medical bills, an inheritance, property purchases, reaching an age where your RMD kicks in or travel, any number of things can affect how much income you report and how many deductions you take each year.

Preparing for the ever-changing landscape of your financial life requires a tax-diversified portfolio that can be leveraged to balance the incomes, expenditures and deductions that affect you each year. A financial professional will work with you to answer questions like these:

- What does your tax landscape look like?

- Do you have a tax-diversified portfolio robust enough to adapt to your needs?
- Do you have a diversity of taxable and non-taxable income planned for your retirement?
- Will you be able to maximize your distributions to take advantage of your deductions when you retire?
- Is your portfolio strong enough and tax-diversified enough to adapt to an ever-changing (and usually increasing) tax code?

> » *When Penny returns home after a week in the hospital recovering from a knee replacement, the 77-year-old calls her daughter, sister and brother to let them know she is home and feeling well. She also should have called her CPA. Penny's medical expenses for the procedure, her hospital stay, her medications and the ongoing physical therapy she attended amount to more than $50,000.*
>
> *Currently, Americans can deduct medical expenses that are more than 7.5 percent of their Adjusted Gross Income (AGI). Penny's AGI is $60,000 the year of her knee replacement, meaning she is able to deduct $44,000 of her medical bills from her taxes that year. Her AGI dictated that she could deduct more than 80 percent of her medical expenses that year.* **Penny didn't know this.**
>
> *Had she been working with a financial professional who regularly asked her about any changes in her life, her spending, or her expenses (expected or unexpected), Penny could have saved thousands of dollars. Penny can also file an amendment to her tax return to recoup the overpayment.*

This relatively simple example of how tax planning can save you money is just the tip of the iceberg. No one can be expected to know the entire U.S. tax code. But a professional who is working with a team of CPAs and financial professionals has an advantage over the average taxpayer who must start from square one on their own every year. Have you been taking advantage of all the deductions that are available to you?

PROACTIVE TAX PLANNING

The implications of proactive tax planning are far reaching, and are larger than many people realize. Remember, doing your taxes in January, February, March or April means you are writing a history book. Planning your taxes in October, November or December means that you are writing the story as it happens. You can look at all the factors that are at play and make decisions that will impact your tax return *before* you file it.

Realizing that tax planning is an aspect of financial planning is an important leap to make. When you incorporate tax planning into your financial planning strategy, it becomes part of the way you maximize your financial potential. Paying less in taxes means you keep more of your money. Simply put, the more money you keep, the more of it you can leverage as an asset. This kind of planning can affect you at any stage of your life. If you are 40 years old, are you contributing the maximum amount to your 401(k) plan? Are you contributing to a Roth IRA? Are you finding ways to structure the savings you are dedicating to your children's education? Do you have life insurance? Taxes and tax planning affect all of these investment tools. Having a relationship with a professional who works with a CPA can help you build a truly comprehensive financial plan that not only works with your investments, but also shapes your assets to find the most efficient ways to prepare for tax time. There may be years that you could benefit from higher distributions because of the tax bracket that you are in, or there could be years you would benefit from taking less. There may be years when you have a lot of deductions and years you have relatively few. **Adapting your distributions to**

work in concert with your available deductions is at the heart of smart tax planning. Professional guidance can bring you to the next level of income distribution, allowing you to remain flexible enough to maximize your tax efficiency. And remember, saving money on taxes makes you more money than making money does.

What you have on paper is important: your assets, savings, investments, which are financial expression of your work and time. It's just as important to know how to get it off the paper in a way that keeps most of it in your pocket. Almost anything that involves financial planning also involves taxes. Annuities, investments, IRAs, 401(k)s, 403(b), and many other investment options will have tax implications. Life also has a way of throwing curveballs. Illness, expensive car repair or replacement, or *any event that has a financial impact on your life will likely have a corresponding tax implication* around which you should adapt your financial plan. Tax planning does just that.

One dollar can end up being less than 25 cents to your heirs.

» *When Leeland's father passed away, he discovered that he was the beneficiary of his father's $500,000 IRA. Leeland has a wife and a family of four children, and he knew that his father had intended for a large portion of the IRA to go toward funding their college educations.*

After Leeland's father's estate is distributed, Leeland, who is 50 years old and whose two oldest sons are entering college, liquidates the IRA. By doing so, his taxable income for that year puts him in a 39.6 percent tax bracket, immediately reducing the value of the asset to $302,000. An additional 3.8 percent surtax on net investment income further diminishes the funds to $283,000. Liquidating the IRA in effect subjects much of Leeland's regular income to the surtax, as well. At this point, Leeland will be taxed at 43.4 percent.

Leeland's state taxes are an additional 9 percent. More-over, estate taxes on Leeland's father's assets claim another 22 percent. By the time the IRS is through, Leeland's income from the IRA will be taxed at 75 percent, leaving him with $125,000 of the original $500,000. While it would help contribute to the education of his children, it wouldn't come anywhere near completely paying for it, something the $500,000 could have easily done.

As the above example makes clear, leaving an asset to your beneficiaries can be more complicated than it may seem. In the case of a traditional IRA, after federal, estate and state taxes, the asset could literally diminish to as little as 25 percent of its value.

How does working with a professional help you make smarter tax decisions with your own finances? Any financial professional worth their salt will be working with a firm that has a team of trained tax professionals, including CPAs, who have an intimate knowledge of the tax code and how to adapt a financial plan to it.

Here's another example of how taxes have major implications on asset management:

» Henry and Alice, a 62-year-old couple, begin working with a financial professional in October. After structuring their assets to reflect their risk tolerance and creating assets that would provide them Safe Money income during retirement, they feel good about their situation. They make decisions that allow them to maximize their Social Security benefits, they have plenty of options for filling their income gap, and they have a strategy in place for emergency funds and growth opportunities. When their professional asks them about their tax plan, they tell him their CPA handled their taxes every year, and did a great job. Their professional says, "I don't mean

who does your taxes, I mean, who does your tax planning?"
Henry and Alice aren't sure how to respond.

Their professional brings Henry and Alice's financial plan
to the firm's CPA and has her run a tax projection for them.
A week later their professional calls them with a tax plan for
the year that will save them more than $3,000 on their tax
return. The couple is shocked. A simple piece of advice from
the CPA based on the numbers revealed that if they paid their
estimated taxes before the end of the year, they would be able
to itemize it as a deduction, allowing them to save thousands
of dollars.

This solution won't work for everyone, and it may not work for
Henry and Alice every year. That's not the point. By being proactive with their approach to taxes and using the resources made
available by their financial professional, they were able to create a
tax plan that saved them money.

ESTATE TAXES

The government doesn't just tax your income from investments
while you're alive. They will also dip into your legacy.

While estate taxes aren't as hot of a topic as they were a few
years ago, they are still an issue of concern for many people with
assets. While taxes may not apply on estates that are less than $5
million, certain states have estate taxes with much lower exclusion
ratios. Some are as low as $600,000. Many people may have to
pay a state estate tax. One strategy for avoiding those types of taxes
is to move assets outside of your estate. That can include gifting
them to family or friends, or putting them into an irrevocable
trust. Life insurance is another option for protecting your legacy.

CHAPTER 8 RECAP //

- When you report your taxes, you are paying to record history. When you *plan* your taxes with a financial professional, you are proactively finding the best options for your tax return. Knowing how to use tax law in your favor means putting more money in your wallet and less money into the hands of Uncle Sam.

- It's important to understand the tax repercussions when tapping into assets from a 401(k) or a traditional IRA for use an income source. Money that is considered qualified by the Federal government must be taxed upon distribution.

- At the age of 70 ½, the Federal Government requires all IRA participants to take their RMD, or Required Minimum Distribution. Failure to take your RMD can cost you thousands of dollars in taxes and penalty fees.

- Taxes play an important role during your retirement. It's important that you understand your obligations, and the differences between tax-deferred and tax-advantaged advantaged accounts.

- You make more money by saving on taxes than you do by making more money. This simple concept becomes extremely valuable to people in retirement and those living on fixed incomes.

9
THE FUTURE OF U.S. TAXATION

Tax legislation over the course of American history has left one very resounding message: taxes go up. Sadly, we hear this same threat so often that it has begun to sound like the boy who cried wolf. The reason behind this lies in the fact that tax hikes usually do not take effect until two or three years after their introduction and subsequently get piecemeal implementation. The result of this prolonged implementation period can be equated to death by a thousand paper cuts.

DEBT CEILING – CAUSE AND EFFECTS
The raising of the debt ceiling raised more than just the ability for our government to go further into debt. It also raised concerns and fears about the future of our economy. We are now seeing

major swings in the markets with investors showing serious concerns over the future of investment valuations and their personal wealth. Unfortunately, the reasoning behind all of this uncertainty is preceded by the inability to see the full implications of what is in store. We rarely talk about the fact that the discussions on raising the debt ceiling were coupled to discussions on major tax reforms needed to correct the problems underlining the debt ceiling increase itself.

Increasing the debt ceiling was needed because the government maxed out its credit card, so to speak, which it has been living off of for quite some time. It is really not much different than what we have been seeing from the general public for the past few decades. Unfortunately, most of us do not have the ability to get a credit limit increase on our credit cards once we reach the maximum limit, that is, unless we can show the ability to pay this balance back. The only way to pay this credit card back is by spending less and making more money.

This is exactly where the federal government is today. They have been given a higher credit limit, but they still must find a way to decrease the spending while making more money. The only way the government makes money is by collecting taxes.

Unfortunately, at the current moment, the government is collecting approximately $120 billion less per month than it currently spends. Discussions for major tax reform have accompanied the discussions for the increased debt ceiling.

DEBT AND EARNINGS

Let us take a closer look at where we are today. The U.S. national debt is increasing at an alarming rate, rising to levels never seen before and threatening serious harm to the economy. Through the end of 2010, the national debt has risen to $13.6 trillion, averaging an 11.4 percent increase annually over the past five years and a 9.2 percent increase annually over the past 10 years. To put this into perspective, the national gross domestic product (GDP) has increased to $14.5 trillion during the same period, averaging a 2.9 percent annual increase over the past five years and a 3.9 percent increase over the past 10 years. At the end of 2010, the national debt level was 93 percent of the GDP. Economists believe that a sustainable economy exists at a maximum level of approximately 80 percent. As of December 20, 2013, the U.S. national debt was 107.69 percent of GDP with the debt at $17.252 trillion and the GDP at $16.020 trillion.*

The significance of these two numbers lies within the contrast. The national debt is the amount that needs to be repaid. This is the credit card balance. Gross domestic product on the other hand is less known and represents the market value of all final goods and services produced within a country during a given period. Essentially, GDP represents the gross taxable income available to the government. If debts are increasing at a greater rate than the gross income available for taxation, then the only way to make up the difference is by increasing the rate at which the gross income is taxed.

The most recent presidential budget shows a continuing trend in the disparity between growth in the national debt and GDP over the next two decades. Although the increasing disparity is a real concern and shows that, at least in the short run, the federal deficit will not be addressed to counteract the potential crisis ahead, it is the revenue collection that tells the disconcerting story. Over the past 40 years the average collection of GDP has been approximately 17.6 percent and currently collections are at approximately 14.4 percent of GDP.

As the presidential budget reveals, the projected revenues are estimated to be 20 percent by the end of the next decade. That is a 38.8 percent increase from the current tax levels. To put this

---

* *http://www.usdebtclock.org/12/20/13*

into perspective, if you are currently in the top tax bracket of 35 percent and this bracket increases by the proposed collection increase, your tax rate will be approximately 48.5 percent. Keep in mind that even at this rate the deficit is projected to increase.

2013 – THE END OF AN ERA?

From a historical point of view, taxes are extremely low. The last time the U.S. national debt was at the same percentage level of GDP as today was at the end of World War II and several years following. The maximum tax rate averaged 90 percent from 1944 through 1963. Compare that to the maximum rate of 35 percent today and it becomes very clear that there is a disparity of extreme proportion.

Taxes during this historical period were at extreme levels for nearly 20 years, during and following this current level of debt-to-GDP. A significant point to note about the difference between that time and today is the economic activity. The period of 1944 through 1963 was in the heart of both the industrial revolution and the birth of the Baby Boom generation. Today, we are mired in extreme volatility with frequent periods of boom and bust at the same time we are witnessing the beginning of the greatest retirement wave ever experienced within the U.S. economy.

To contrast these two time periods in respect to the recovery period is almost asinine as the external pressures from globalization and domestic unfunded liabilities did not exist or were irrelevant factors during the prior period.

To add insult to injury, U.S. domestic unfunded liabilities are currently estimated somewhere around $61.6 trillion due to items such as Social Security, Medicare and government pensions. The most concerning part of this pertains to the coming wave of retirement as the Baby Boom generation begins retiring and drawing on the unfunded Social Security for which they currently have entitlement. Over the long run, expenditures related to healthcare programs such as Medicare and Medicaid are projected to grow faster than the economy overall as the population matures.

To put unfunded liabilities into perspective, consider these as off-balance-sheet obligations similar to those of Enron. Although these are not listed as part of the national debt, they must be paid. These liabilities exist outside of the annual budgetary debt discussed. The difference between Enron and the U.S. unfunded liabilities is that if the U.S. government cannot come up with the funds to pay all these liabilities through revenue generation, they will print the money necessary to pay the debt.

WHAT DOES THE SOLUTION LOOK LIKE?

Unfortunately, the general public is in a no-win situation for this solution to the problem. Printing money does not bode well for economic growth. This creates inflationary pressures that devalue the U.S. dollar and make everyone less wealthy. Cutting the entitlements that compose this liability leaves millions of people without benefits they have come to expect. The only other option, and one that the government knows all too well, is increasing taxes. In fact, according to a Congressional Budget Office paper issued in 2004:

"The term 'unfunded liability' has been used to refer to a gap between the government's projected financial commitment under a particular program and the revenues that are expected to be available to fund that commitment. But no government obligation can be truly considered 'unfunded' because of the U.S. government's sovereign power to tax—which is the ultimate resource to meet its obligations."

A balanced budget will be required at some point and with this will come higher taxes. We have uncertainty surrounding tax rates and how high they will go. At that time, extensions put in place in December 2010 on Bush-era tax cuts are set to expire. We are likely to see some tax increases at this point. Whether it is only on the top earners or unilaterally across all income levels is yet to be seen, but an increase of some sort will most certainly occur.

How do you prepare? Why spend so much time reassuring you that taxes will increase? Because you have an opportunity to take action. Now is the time to prepare for what will come and structure countermeasures for the good, the bad and the ugly of each of these legislative nightmares through tax-advantaged retirement planning.

You make more money by saving on taxes than you do by making more money. The simplistic logic of the statement makes sense when you discover it takes $1.50 in earnings to put that same dollar, saved in taxes, back in your pocket.

As simple as it sounds, it is much more difficult to execute. Most people fail to put together a plan as they near retirement, beginning with a simple cash flow budget. If you have not analyzed your proposed income streams and expenses, you could not possibly have taken the time to position these cash flows and other events into a tax-preferred plan.

Most people will state that they have a plan and, thus, do not need any further assistance in this area. The truth in most instances is that people could not show you their plan, and among the few that could, most would not be able to show you how they have executed it. In this regard, they might as well be Richard Nixon stating, "I am not a crook" for as much as they state, "I have a plan." The truth lies in waiting. As we approach or begin retirement, we should look at what cash flows we will have. Do we have a pension? How about Social Security? How much additional cash flow am I going to need to draw from my assets to maintain the lifestyle that I desire?

We spend our whole lives saving and accumulating wealth but spend so little time determining how to distribute this accumulation so as to retain it. We need to make sure we have the appropriate diversification of taxable versus non-taxable assets to complement our distribution strategy.

THE BENEFITS OF DIVERSIFICATION

Heading into retirement, we should be situated with a dia c c u - mulating wealth is not to see the size of the number on paper, but rather to be an exercise in how much we put in our pocket after removing it from the paper. To truly understand tax diversification, we must understand what types of money exist and how each of these will be treated during accumulation and, most importantly, during distribution. The following is a brief summary:

1. Free money
2. Tax-advantaged money
3. Tax-deferred money
4. Taxable money
   a. Ordinary income
   b. Capital gains and qualified dividends

FREE MONEY

Free money is the best kind of money regardless of tax treatment because, in the end, you have more money than you would have otherwise. Many employers will provide contributions toward employee retirement accounts to offer additional employment benefits and encourage employees to save for their own retirement. With this, employers often will offer a matching contribution in which they contribute up to a certain percentage of an employee's salary (generally three to five percent) toward that employee's retirement account when the employee contributes to their retirement account as well. For example, if an employee earns $50,000 annually and contributes three percent ($1,500) to their retirement account annually, the employer will also contribute three percent ($1,500) to the employee's account. That is $1,500 in free money. Take all you can get! Bear in mind that any employer contribution to a 401(k) will still be subject to taxation when withdrawn.

TAX-ADVANTAGED MONEY

Tax-advantaged money is the next best thing to free money. Although you have to earn tax-advantaged money, you do not have to give part of it away to Uncle Sam. Tax-advantaged money comes in three basic forms that you can utilize during your lifetime; four if prison inspires your future, but we are not going to discuss that option.

One of the most commonly known forms of tax-advantaged money is municipal bonds, which earn and pay interest that could be tax-advantaged on the federal level, or state level, or both. There are several caveats that should be discussed with regard to the notion of tax-advantaged income from municipal bonds. First, you will notice that tax-advantaged has several flavors from the state and federal perspective. This is because states will generally tax the interest earned on a municipal bond unless the bond is offered from an entity located within that state. This severely limits the availability of completely tax-advantaged municipal bonds and constrains underlying risk and liquidity factors. Second, municipal bond interest is added back into the equation for determining your modified adjusted gross income (MAGI) for Social Security. This could push your income above a threshold and subject a portion of your Social Security income to taxation.

In effect, if this interest subjects some other income to taxation then this interest is truly being taxed.

Last, municipal bond interest may be excluded from the regular federal tax system, but it is included for determining tax under the alternative minimum tax (AMT) system. In its basic form, the AMT system is a separate tax system that applies if the tax computed under AMT exceeds the tax computed under the regular tax system. The difference between these two computations is the alternative minimum tax.

TAX-ADVANTAGED MONEY: ROTH IRA

Roth accounts are probably the single greatest tax asset that has come from Congress. They are well known but rarely used. Roth IRAs were first established by the Taxpayer Relief Act of 1997 and named after Senator William Roth, the chief sponsor of the legislation. Roth accounts are simply an account in the form of an individual retirement account or an employer sponsored retirement account that allows for tax-advantaged growth of earnings and, thus, tax-advantaged income.

The main difference between a Roth and a traditional IRA or employer-sponsored plan lies in the timing of the taxation. We are all very familiar with the typical scenario of putting money away for retirement through an employer plan, whereby they deduct money from our paychecks and put it directly into a retirement account. This money is taken out before taxes are calculated, meaning we do not pay tax on those earnings today. A Roth account, on the other hand, takes the money after the taxes have been removed and puts it into the retirement account, so we do pay tax on the money today. The other significant difference between these two is taxation during distribution in later years. Regarding our traditional retirement accounts, when we take the money out later it is added to our ordinary income and is taxed accordingly. Additionally, including this in our income subjects us to the consequences mentioned above for municipal bonds with Social Security taxation, AMT, as well as higher Medicare premiums. A Roth on the other hand is distributed tax-advantaged and does not contribute toward negative impact items such as Social Security taxation, AMT, or Medicare premium increases. It essentially comes back to us without tax and other obligations.

The best way to view the difference between the two accounts is to look at the life of a farmer. A farmer will buy seed, plant it in the ground, grow the crops and harvest it later for sale. Typically, the farmer would only pay tax on the crops that have been harvested and sold. But if you were the farmer, would you rather pay tax on the $5,000 of seed that you plant today or the $50,000 of crops harvested later? The obvious answer is $5,000 of seed today. The truth to the matter is that you are a farmer, except you plant dollars into your retirement account instead of seeds into the earth.

So why doesn't everyone have a Roth retirement account if things are so simple? There are several reasons, but the single greatest reason has been the constraints on contributions. If you earned over certain thresholds (MAGI over $125,000 single and $183,000 joint for 2012), you were not eligible to make contributions, and until last year, if your modified adjusted gross income (MAGI) was over $100,000 (single or joint), you could not convert a traditional IRA to a Roth. Outside these contribution limits, most people save for retirement through their employers and most employers do not offer Roth options in their plans. The reason behind this is because Roth accounts are not that well understood and people have been educated to believe that saving on taxes today is the best possible course of action.

TAX-DEFERRED MONEY

Tax-deferred money is the type of money with which most of people are familiar, but we also briefly reviewed the idea above. Tax-deferred money is typically our traditional IRA, employer sponsored retirement plan or a non-qualified annuity. Essentially, you put money into an investment vehicle that will accumulate in value over time and you do not pay taxes on the earnings that grow these accounts until you distribute them. Once the money is distributed, taxes must be paid. However, the same negative consequences exist with regard to additional taxation and expense in other areas as previously discussed. The cash accumulation value can be used for tax-advantaged income.

TAXABLE MONEY

Taxable money is everything else and is taxable today, later or whenever it is received. These four types of money come down to two distinct classifications: taxable and tax-free. The greatest difference when comparing taxable and tax-advantaged income is a function of how much money we keep after tax. For help in determining what the differences should be, excluding outside factors such as Social Security taxation and AMT, a tax equivalent yield should be used.

TAX-ADVANTAGED IN THE REAL WORLD

To put the tax equivalent yield into perspective, let us look at an example: Rick and Mary are currently retired, living on Social Security and interest from investments and falling within the 25 percent tax bracket. They have a substantial portion of their investments in municipal bonds yielding 6 percent, which is quite comforting in today's market. The tax equivalent yield they would need to earn from a taxable investment would be 8 percent, a 2 percent gap that seems almost impossible given current market volatility. However, something that has never been put into perspective is that the interest from their municipal bonds is subject to taxation on their Social Security benefits (at 21.25 percent). With this, the yield on their municipal bonds would be 4.725percent, and the taxable equivalent yield falls to 6.3 percent, leaving a gap of only 1.575 percent.

In the end, most people spend their lives accumulating wealth through the best, if not the only vehicle they know, a tax-deferred account. This account is most likely a 401(k) or 403(b) plan offered through our employer and may be supplemented with an

IRA that was established at one point or another. As the years go by, people blindly throw money into these accounts in an effort to save for a retirement that we someday hope to reach.

The truth is, most people have an age selected for when they would like to retire, but spend their lives wondering if they will ever be able to actually quit working. To answer this question, you must understand how much money you will have available to contribute toward your needs. *In other words, you need to know what your after-tax income will be during this period.*

All else being equal, it would not matter if you put your money into a taxable, tax-deferred or tax-advantaged account as long as income tax rates never change and outside factors are never an event. The net amount you receive in the end will be the same.

Unfortunately, this will never be the case. We already know that taxes will increase in the future, meaning we will likely see higher taxes in retirement than during our peak earning years.

Regardless, saving for retirement in any form is a good thing as it appears from all practical perspectives that future government benefits will be cut and taxes will increase. You have the ability to plan today for efficient tax diversification and maximization of our after-tax dollars during your distribution years.

CHAPTER 9 RECAP //

- A closer examination of the debt ceiling and taxes through-out U.S. history points to the benefits of tax diversification.
- Most people are familiar with tax-deferred methods of retirement savings such a traditional IRAs. By taking action now, you can prepare for the rise in taxes by restructuring your assets to include the benefits of free and tax-advantaged money.
- Tax-advantaged money is money you earn without having to pay taxes on. One of the most common forms includes municipal bonds, but be aware these come with many state and federal caveats and complexities.
- Roth IRAs and life insurance are two forms of tax-advantaged money that can take advantage of today's lower tax rate when preparing for tomorrow's retirement.

10

GET IT WHILE IT'S ON SALE:

TAXES AND YOUR ROTH IRA

Louis Brandeis provides one of the best examples illustrating how tax planning works. Brandeis was Associate Justice on the Supreme Court of the United States from 1916 to 1939. Born in Louisville, Kentucky, Brandeis was an intelligent man with a touch of country charm. He described tax planning this way:

"I live in Alexandria, Virginia. Near the Court Chambers, there is a toll bridge across the Potomac. When in a rush, I pay the dollar toll and get home early. However, I usually drive outside the downtown section of the city and cross the Potomac on a free bridge.

The bridge was placed outside the downtown Washington, D.C. area to serve a useful social service—getting drivers to drive the extra mile and help alleviate congestion during the rush hour.

If I went over the toll bridge and through the barrier without paying a toll, I would be committing tax evasion.

If I drive the extra mile and drive outside the city of Washington to the free bridge, I am using a legitimate, logical and suitable method of tax avoidance, and I am performing a useful social service by doing so.

*The tragedy is that **few people know that the free bridge exists.** "*

Like Brandeis, most American taxpayers have options when it comes to "crossing the Potomac," so to speak. It's a financial planner's job to tell you what options are available. You can wait until March to file your taxes, at which time you might pay someone to report and pay the government a larger portion of your income. However, you could instead file before the end of the year, work with your financial professional and incorporat CHRe a tax plan as part of your overall financial planning strategy. Filing later is like crossing the toll bridge. Tax planning is like crossing the free bridge.

Which would you rather do?

The answer to this question is easy. Most people want to save money and pay less in taxes. What makes this situation really difficult in real life, however, is that the signs along the side of the road that direct us to the free bridge are not that clear. To normal Americans, and to plenty of people who have studied it, the U.S. tax code is easy to get lost in. There are all kinds of rules, exceptions to rules, caveats and conditions that are difficult to understand, or even to know about. What you really need to know is your options and the bottom line impacts of those options.

ROTH IRA CONVERSIONS

The attractive qualities of Roth IRAs may have prompted you to explore the possibility of moving some of your assets into a Roth account. Another important difference between the accounts is how they treat Required Minimum Distributions (RMDs). When you turn 70 ½ years old, you are required to take a minimum amount of money out of a traditional IRA. This amount is your RMD. It is treated as taxable income. Roth IRAs, however, do not have RMDs, and their distributions are not taxable. Quite a deal, right?

While having a Roth IRA as part of your portfolio is a good idea, converting assets to a Roth IRA can pose some challenges, depending on what kinds of assets you want to transfer. The success of your conversion will all depend on the timing.

You may have heard about converting your IRA to a Roth IRA, but you might not know the full net result on your income. The main difference between the two accounts is that the growth of investments within a traditional IRA is not taxed until income is withdrawn from the account, whereas taxes are charged on contribution amounts to a Roth IRA, not withdrawals. The problem, however, is that when assets are removed from a traditional IRA, even if the assets are being transferred to a Roth IRA account, taxes apply.

There are a lot of reasons to look at Roth conversions. People have a lot of money in IRAs, up to multiple millions of dollars. Even with $500,000, when they turn 70 ½ years old, their RMD is going to be approximately $18,000, and they have to take that out whether they want to or not. It's a tax issue. Essentially, if you will be subject to high RMDs, it could have impacts on how much of your Social Security is taxable, and on your tax bracket.

By paying taxes now instead of later on assets in a Roth IRA, you can realize tax-advantaged growth. You pay once and you're done paying. Your heirs are done paying. It's a powerful tool. Here's a simple example to show you how powerful it can be:

Imagine that you pay to convert a traditional IRA to a Roth. You have decided that you want to put the money in a vehicle that gives you a tax-advantaged income option down the road. If you pay a

25 percent tax on that conversion and the Roth IRA then doubles in value over the next 10 years, you could look at your situation as only having paid 12.5 percent tax.

The prospect of tax-advantaged income is a tempting one. While you have to pay a conversion tax to transfer your assets, you also have turned taxable income into tax free retirement money that you can let grow as long as you want without being required to withdraw it.

There are options, however, that address this problem. Much like the Brandeis story, there may be a "free bridge" option for many investors.

Your financial professional will likely tell you that it is not a matter of whether or not you should perform a Roth IRA conversion, it is a matter of how much you should convert and when.

Here are some of the things to consider before converting to a Roth IRA:

If you make a conversion before you retire, you may end up paying higher taxes on the conversion because it is likely that you are in some of your highest earning years, placing you in the highest tax bracket of your life. It is possible that a better strategy would be to wait until after you retire, a time when you may have less taxable income, which would place you in a lower tax bracket.

Many people opt to reduce their work hours from fulltime to part-time in the years before they retire. If you have pursued this option, your income will likely be lower, in turn lowering your tax rate.

The first years that you draw Social Security benefits can also be years of lower reported income, making it another good time frame in which to convert to a Roth IRA.

One key strategy to handling a Roth IRA conversion is to **always be able to pay the cost of the tax conversion with outside money**. Structuring your tax year to include something like a significant deduction can help you offset the conversion tax. This way you aren't forced to take the money you need for taxes from the value of the IRA. The reason taxes apply to this maneuver is because when you withdraw money from a traditional IRA, it is treated as taxable income by the IRS. Your financial professional, with the help of the CPAs at their firm, may be able to provide you with options like after-tax money, itemized deductions or other situations that can pose effective tax avoidance options.

Some examples of avoiding Roth IRA conversions taxes include:

- *Using medical expenses that are above 10 percent of your Adjusted Gross Income.* If you have health care costs that you can list as itemized deductions, you can convert an amount of income from a traditional IRA to a Roth IRA that is offset by the deductible amount. Essentially, deductible medical expenses negate the taxes resulting from recording the conversion.

- *Individuals, usually small business owners, who are dealing with a Net Operating Loss (NOL).* If you have NOLs, but aren't able to utilize all of them on your tax return, you can carry them forward to offset the taxable income from the taxes on income you convert to a Roth IRA.

- *Charitable giving.* If you are charitably inclined, you can use the amount of your donations to reduce the amount of taxable income you have during that year. By matching the amount you convert to a Roth IRA to the amount your taxable income was reduced by charitable giving, you can essentially avoid taxation on the conversion. You may decide to double your donations to a charity in one year, giving them two years' worth of donations in order to offset the Roth IRA conversion tax on this year's tax return.

- *Investments that are subject to depletion.* Certain investments can kick off depletion expenses. If you make an investment and are subject to depletion expenses, they can be deducted and used to offset a Roth IRA conversion tax.

Not all of the above scenarios work for everyone, and there are many other options for offsetting conversion taxes. The point is that you have options, and your financial professional and tax professional can help you understand those options.

If you have a traditional IRA, Roth conversions are something you should look at. As you approach retirement you should consider your options and make choices that keep more of your money in your pocket, not the government's.

ADDITIONAL TAX BENEFITS OF ROTH IRAS

Not only do Roth IRAs provide you with tax-advantaged growth, they also give you a tax diversified landscape that allows you to maximize your distributions. Chances are that no matter the circumstances, you will have taxed income and other assets subject to taxation. *But if you have a Roth IRA, you have the unique ability to manage your Adjusted Gross Income (AGI), because you have a tax-advantaged income option!*

Converting to a Roth IRA can also help you preserve and build your legacy. Because Roth IRAs are exempt from RMDs, after you make a conversion from a traditional IRA, your Roth account can grow tax-advantaged for another 15, 20 or 25 years and it can be used as tax-advantaged income by your heirs. It is important to note, however, that non-spousal beneficiaries do have to take

RMDs from a Roth IRA, or choose to stretch it and draw tax-advantaged income out of it over their lifetime.

TO CONVERT OR NOT TO CONVERT?

Conversions aren't only for retirees. You can convert at any time. Your choice should be based on your individual circumstances and tax situation. Sticking with a traditional IRA or converting to a Roth, again, depends on your individual circumstances, including your income, your tax bracket and the amount of deductions you have each year.

Is it better to have a Roth IRA or traditional IRA? It depends on your individual circumstance. Some people don't mind having taxable income from an IRA. Their income might not be very high and their RMD might not bump their tax bracket up, so it's not as big a deal. A similar situation might involve income from Social Security. Social Security benefits are taxed based on other income you are drawing. If you are in a position where none or very little of your Social Security benefit is subject to taxes, paying income tax on your RMD may be very easy.

> » *There are also situations where leveraging taxable income from a traditional IRA can work to your advantage come tax time. For example, Bob and Ashely dream of buying a boat when they retire. It is something they have looked forward to their entire marriage. In addition to the savings and investments that they created to supply them with income during retirement, which includes a traditional IRA, they have also saved money for the sole purpose of purchasing a boat once they stop working.*
>
> *When the time comes and they finally buy the boat of their dreams, they pay an additional $15,000 in sales taxes that year because of the large purchase. Because they are retired and earning less money, the deductions they used to be able to*

realize from their income taxes are no longer there. The high amount of sales taxes they paid on the boat puts them in a position where they could benefit from taking taxable income from a traditional IRA.

When Bob and Ashley's financial professional learns about their purchase, he immediately contacts a CPA at his firm to run the numbers. They determine that by taking a $15,000 distribution from their IRA, they could fulfill their income needs to offset the $15,000 sales tax deduction that they were claiming due to the purchase of their boat. In the end, they pay zero taxes on their income distribution from their IRA.

The moral of the story? **Having a tax diversified landscape gives you options.** Having capital assets that can be liquidated, tax-advantaged income options and sources that can create capital gains or capital losses will put you in a position to play your cards right no matter what you want to accomplish with your taxes. The ace up your sleeve is your financial professional and the CPAs they work with. Do yourself a favor and *plan* your taxes instead of *reporting* them!

CHAPTER 10 RECAP //

- Look for the "free bridge" option in your tax strategy.
- Converting from a traditional to a Roth IRA can provide you with tax-advantaged retirement income.
- Converting to a Roth IRA can also help you preserve and build your legacy.
- There are many ways to reduce your taxes. Being smart about your Roth IRA conversion is one of the main ways to do so.

11

YOUR LEGACY BEYOND DOLLARS AND CENTS

If you're like most people, planning your estate isn't on the top of your list of things to do. Planning your income needs for retirement, managing your assets and just living your life without worrying about how your estate will be handled when you are gone make legacy planning less than attractive for a Saturday afternoon task. The fact of the matter, however, is that if you don't plan your legacy, someone else will. That someone else is usually a combination of the IRS and other government entities: lawyers, executors, courts, and accountants. Who do you think has the best interests of your beneficiaries in mind?

Today, there is more consideration given to planning a legacy than just maximizing your estate. When most people think about an estate, it may seem like something only the very wealthy have: a stately manor or an enormous business. But a legacy is something else entirely. A legacy is more than the sum total of the financial assets you have accumulated. It is the lasting impression you make on those you leave behind. The dollar and cents are just a small part of a legacy.

A legacy encompasses the stories that others tell about you, shared experiences and values. An estate may pay for college tuition, but a legacy may inform your grandchildren about the importance of higher education and self-reliance.

A legacy may also contain family heirlooms or items of emotional significance. It may be a piece of art your great-grandmother painted, family photos, or a childhood keepsake.

When you go about planning your legacy, certainly explore strategies that can maximize the financial benefit to the ones you care about. But also take the time to ensure that you have organized the whole of your legacy, and let that be a part of the last gift you leave.

Many people avoid planning their legacy until they feel they must. Something may change in your life, like the birth of a grandchild, the diagnosis of a serious health problem, or the death of a close friend or loved one. Waiting for tragedy to strike in order to get your affairs in order is not the best course of action. The emotional stress of that kind of situation can make it hard to make patient, thoughtful decisions. Taking the time to create a premeditated and thoughtful legacy plan will assure that your assets will be transferred where and when you want them when the time comes.

THE BENEFITS OF PLANNING YOUR LEGACY

The distribution of your assets, whether in the form of property, stocks, Individual Retirement Accounts, 401(k)s or liquid assets, can be a complicated undertaking if you haven't left clear instructions about how you want them handled. Not having a plan will cost more money and take more time, leaving your loved ones to wait (sometimes for years) and receive less of your legacy than if you had a clear plan.

Planning your legacy will help your assets be transferred with little delay and little confusion. Instead of leaving decisions about how to distribute your estate to your family, attorneys or financial professionals, preserve your legacy and your wishes by drafting a clear plan at an early age.

And while you know all that, it can still be hard to sit down and do it. It reminds you that life is short, and the relatively complicated nature of sorting through your assets can feel like a daunting task. But one thing is for sure: *it is impossible for your assets to be transferred or distributed the way you want at the end of your life if you don't have a plan.*

Ask yourself:

- Are my assets up to date?
- Have my primary and contingent beneficiaries been clearly designated?
- Does my plan allow for restriction of a beneficiary?
- Does my legacy plan address minor children that I want to provide with income?
- Does my legacy plan allow for multi-generational payout?

Answers to these questions are critical if you want the final say in how your assets are distributed. In order to achieve your legacy goals, you need a plan.

MAKING A PLAN

Eventually, when your income need is filled and you have sufficient standby money to meet your need for emergencies, travel or other extra expenses you are planning for, whatever isn't used during your lifetime becomes your financial legacy. The money that you do not use during your lifetime will either go to loved ones, unloved ones, charity, or the IRS. The questions is, who would you rather disinherit?

By having a legacy plan that clearly outlines your assets, your beneficiaries and your distribution goals, you can make sure that your money and property is ending up in the hands of the people you determine beforehand. Is it really that big of a deal? It absolutely is. Think about it. Without a clear plan, it is impossible for anyone to know if your beneficiary designations are current and reflect your wishes because you haven't clearly expressed who your beneficiaries are. You may have an idea of who you want your assets to go to, but without a plan, it is anyone's guess. It is also impossible to know if the titling of your assets is accurate unless you have gone through and determined whose name is on the titles. More importantly, *if you have not clearly and effectively communicated your desires regarding the planned distribution of your legacy, you and your family may end up losing a large part of it.*

As you can see, managing a legacy is more complicated than having an attorney read your will, divide your estate and write checks to your heirs. The additional issue of taxes, Family Maximum Benefit calculations and a host of other decisions rear their heads. Educating yourself about the best options for positioning your legacy assets is a challenging undertaking. Working with a financial professional who is versed in determining the most efficient and effective ways of preserving and distributing your legacy can save you time, money and strife.

So, how do you begin?

Making a Legacy Plan Starts with a Simple List. The first, and one of the largest, steps to setting up an estate plan with a financial professional that reflects your desires is creating a detailed inventory of your assets and debts (if you have any). You need to know what assets you have, who the beneficiaries are, how much they are worth and how they are titled. You can start by identifying and listing your assets. This is a good starting point for working with a financial professional who can then help you determine the detailed information about your assets that will dictate how they are distributed upon your death.

If you are particularly concerned about leaving your kids and grandkids a lifetime of income with minimal taxes, you will want to discuss a Stretch IRA option with your financial professional.

STRETCH IRAS: GETTING THE MOST OUT OF YOUR MONEY

In 1986, the U.S. Congress passed a law that allows for multi-generational distributions of IRA assets. This type of distribution is called a Stretch IRA because it stretches the distribution of the account out over a longer period of time to several beneficiaries. It also allows the account to continue accumulating value throughout your relatives' lifetimes. You can use a Stretch IRA as an income tool that distributes throughout your lifetime, your children's lifetimes and your grandchildren's lifetimes.

Stretch IRAs are an attractive option for those more concerned with creating income for their loved ones than leaving them with a lump sum that may be subject to a high tax rate. With traditional IRA distributions, non-spousal beneficiaries must generally take distributions from their inherited IRAs, whether transferred or not, within five years after the death of the IRA owner. An exception to this rule applies if the beneficiary elects to take distributions over his or her lifetime, which is referred to as stretching the IRA.

Let's begin by looking at the potential of stretching an IRA throughout multiple generations.

> » *In this scenario, Mr. Cleaver has an IRA with a current balance of $350,000. If we assume a five percent annual rate of return, and a 28 percent tax rate, the Stretch IRA turned*

a $502,625 legacy into more than $1.5 million. Doubling the value of the IRA also provided Mr. Cleaver, his wife, two children and three grandchildren with income. Not choosing the stretch option would have cost nearly $800,000 and had impacts on six of Mr. Cleaver's loved ones.

Unfortunately, many things may also play a role in failing to stretch IRA distributions. It can be tempting for a beneficiary to take a lump sum of money despite the tax consequences. Fortunately, if you want to solidify your plan for distribution, there are

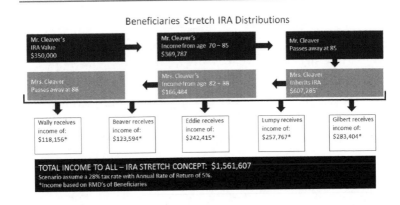

Beneficiaries Stretch IRA Distributions

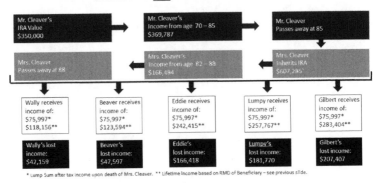

Beneficiaries **FAIL** to Stretch IRA Distributions

options that will allow you to open up an IRA and incorporate "spendthrift" clauses for your beneficiaries. This will ensure your legacy is stretched appropriately and to your specifications. Only certain insurance companies allow this option, and you will not find this benefit with any brokerage accounts. You need to work with a financial professional who has the appropriate relationship with an insurance company that provides this option.

CHAPTER 11 RECAP //

- Your legacy encompasses more than just the physical assets left behind for your children, grandchildren and charities or organizations. It's how you will be remembered.
- Managing a legacy is more complicated than having an attorney read your will, divide your estate, and write checks to your heirs. Issues such as taxes, Family Maximum Benefit calculations and a host of other concerns make it necessary to educate yourself. Working with a financial professional can save you time, money and stress.
- Legacy planning begins with a simple list.

12
PREPARING YOUR LEGACY

Harvey organized his assets long ago. He started planning his retirement early and made investment decisions that would meet his needs. With a combination of IRA to Roth IRA conversions, a series of income annuities and a well-planned money management strategy overseen by his financial professional, he easily filled his income gap and was able to focus on ways to accumulate his wealth throughout his retirement. He reorganized his Risk Money and Safe Money as he got older. When Harvey retired, he had an income plan created that allowed him to maximize his Social Security benefit. He even had enough to accumulate wealth during his retirement. At this point, Harvey turned his attention to planning his legacy. He wanted to know how he could maximize the amount of his legacy he will pass on to his heirs.

Harvey met with an attorney to draw up a will, but he quickly learned that while having a will was a good plan, it wasn't the most efficient way to distribute his legacy. In fact, relying solely on a will created several roadblocks.

The two main problems that arose for Harvey were *Probate* and *Unintentional Disinheritance:*

Problem #1: Probate

Probate. Just speaking the word out loud can cause shivers to run down your spine. Probate's ugly reputation is well deserved. It can be a costly, time consuming process that diminishes your estate and can delay the distribution of your estate to your loved ones. Nasty stuff, by any measure. Unless you have made a clear legacy plan and discussed options for avoiding probate, it is highly likely that you have many assets that might pass through probate needlessly. ***If your will and beneficiary designations aren't correctly structured, some of these assets will go through the probate process, which can turn dollars into cents.***

If you have a will, probate is usually just a formality. There is little risk that your will won't be executed per your instructions. The problem arises when the costs and lengthy timeline that probate creates come into play. Probate proceedings are notoriously expensive, lengthy and ponderous. A typical probate process identifies all of your assets and debts, pays any taxes and fees that you owe (including estate tax), pays court fees, and distributes your property and assets to your heirs. This process usually takes at least a year, and can take even longer before your heirs actually receive anything that you have left for them. For this reason, and because of the sometimes exorbitant fees that may be charged by lawyers and accountants during the process, probate has earned a nasty reputation.

Probate can also be a painstakingly public process. Because the probate process happens in court, the assets you own that go through a probate procedure become part of the public record. While this may not seem like a big deal to some, other people don't want that kind of intimate information available to the public.

Additionally, if your estate is entirely distributed via your will, the money that your family may need to cover the costs of your medical bills, funeral expenses and estate taxes will be tied up in probate, which can last up to a year or more. While immediate family members may have the option of requesting immediate cash from your assets during probate to cover immediate health care expenses, taxes, and fees, that process comes with its own set of complications. Choosing alternative methods for distributing your legacy can make life easier for your loved ones and can help them claim more of your estate in a more timely fashion than traditional methods.

A simpler and less tedious approach is to avoid probate altogether by structuring your estate to be distributed outside of the probate process. Two common ways of doing this are by structuring your assets inside a life insurance plan, and by using individual retirement planning tools like IRAs that give you the option of designating a beneficiary upon your death.

Problem #2: Unintentionally Disinheriting Your Family

You would never want to unintentionally disinherit a loved one or loved ones because of confusion surrounding your legacy plan. Unfortunately, it happens. Why? This terrible situation is typically caused by a simple lack of understanding. In particular, mistakes regarding legacy distribution occur with regards to those whom people care for the most: their grandchildren.

One of the most important ways to plan for the inheritance of your grandchildren is by properly structuring the distribution of your legacy. Specifically, you need to know if your legacy is going to be distributed *per stirpes* or *per capita*.

Per Stirpes. *Per stirpes* is a legal term in Latin that means "by the branch." Your estate will be distributed *per stirpes* if you designate each branch of your family to receive an equal share of your estate. In the event that your children predecease you, their share will be distributed evenly between their children—your grandchildren.

Per Capita. *Per capita* distribution is different in that you may designate different amounts of your estate to be distributed to members of the same generation.

Per stirpes distribution of assets will follow the family tree down the line as the predecessor beneficiaries pass away. On the other hand, per capita distribution of assets ends on the branch of the family tree with the death of a designated beneficiary. For example, when your child passes away, in a per capita distribution, your grandchildren would not receive distributions from the assets that you designated to your child.

What the terms mean is not nearly as important as what they do, however. The reality is that improperly titled assets could accidentally leave your grandchildren disinherited upon the death of their parents. It's easy to check, and it's even easier to fix.

A simple way to remember the difference between the two types of distribution goes something like this: "***Stirpes are forever and Capita is capped.***"

Another way to avoid complicated legacy distribution problems, and the probate process, is by leveraging a life insurance plan.

LIFE INSURANCE: AN IMPORTANT LEGACY TOOL

One of the most powerful legacy tools you can leverage is a good life insurance policy. Life insurance is a highly efficient legacy tool because it creates money when it is needed or desired the most. Over the years, life insurance has become less expensive, while it offers more features, and it provides longer guarantees.

There are many unique benefits of life insurance that can help your beneficiaries get the most out of your legacy. Some of them include:

- Providing beneficiaries with a tax-free, liquid asset.
- Covering the costs associated with your death.
- Providing income for your dependents.
- Offering an investment opportunity for your beneficiaries.
- Covering expenses such as tuition or mortgage down payments for your children or grandchildren.

Very few people want life insurance, but nearly everyone wants what it does. Life insurance is specifically, and uniquely, capable of creating money when it is needed most. When a loved one passes, no amount of money can remove the pain of loss. And certainly, money doesn't solve the challenges that might arise with losing someone important.

It has been said that when you have money, you have options. When you don't have money, your options are severely limited. You might imagine a life insurance policy can give your family and loved ones options that would otherwise be impossible.

> » *Rick spent the last 20 years building a small business. In so many ways, it is a family business. Each of his three children, Maddie, Ruby and Edward, worked in the shop part-time during high school. But after all three attended college, only Maddie returned to join her father, and eventually will run the business full-time when Rick retires.*
>
> *Rick is able to retire comfortably on Social Security and on-going income from the shop, but the business is nearly his entire financial legacy. It is his wish that Maddie own the business outright, but he also wants to leave an equal legacy to each of his three children.*

There is no simple way to divide the business into thirds and still leave the business intact for Maddie.

Rick ends up buying a life insurance policy to make up the difference. Ruby and Edward will receive their share of an inheritance in cash from the life insurance policy and Maddie will be able to inherit the business intact.

Rick is able to accomplish his goals, treat all three children equitably and leave Maddie the business she helped to build.

If you have a life insurance policy but you haven't looked at it in a while, you may not know how it operates, how much it is worth and how it will be distributed to your beneficiaries. You may also need to update your beneficiaries on your policy. In short, without a comprehensive review of your policy, you don't really know where the money will go or to whom it will go.

If you don't have a life insurance policy but are looking for options to maintain and grow your legacy, speaking with a professional can show you the benefits of life insurance. Many people don't consider buying a life insurance policy until some event in their life triggers it, like the loss of a loved one, an accident or a health condition.

BENEFITS OF LIFE INSURANCE

Life insurance is a useful and secure tool for contingency planning, ensuring that your dependents receive the assets that you want them to have, and for meeting the financial goals you have set for the future. While it bears the name "Life Insurance," it is, in reality, a diverse financial tool that can meet many needs. The main function of a life insurance policy is to provide financial assets for your survivors. Life insurance is particularly efficient at achieving this goal because it provides a tax-advantaged lump sum of money in the form of a death benefit to your beneficiary or beneficiaries. That financial asset can be used in a number of ways. It can be structured as an investment to provide income for your spouse or children, it can pay down debts, and it can be used to cover estate taxes and other costs associated with death.

Living Benefits:

Many of today's life insurance policies and annuity products also have riders and provisions for increased income in the event of chronic illness. Often known as Living Benefits, these products provide you with the means to pay for home health care or a nursing home facility while you are still alive. With annuities, these benefits are sometimes known as "income doublers" because the fixed income contracted by the rider will double should you or your spouse require long term care. Long term care can include basic custodial services such as cleaning and taking out the garbage, or it can be more involved and include intrinsic nursing services. Even if it's too late to qualify for traditional long term care insurance, long term care riders on annuity and life insurance products might still be an option for you, and if you never need long term care, that money is not lost. Instead, your beneficiaries receive a legacy.

Tax Benefits:

Tax liabilities on the estate you leave behind are inevitable. Capital property, for instance, is taxed at its fair market value at the time of your death, unless that property is transferred to your spouse. If the property has appreciated during the time you owned it, taxation on capital gains will occur. Registered Retirement Savings Plans (RRSPs) and other similarly structured assets are also included as taxable income unless transferred to a beneficiary as well. Those are just a few examples of how an estate can become subject to a heavy tax burden. The unique benefits of a life insurance policy provide ways to handle this tax burden, solving any liquidity problems that may arise if your family members want to hold onto an illiquid asset, such as a piece of property or an investment. Life insurance can provide a significant amount of money to a family member or other beneficiary, and that money is likely to remain exempt from taxation or seizure.

Protection Benefits:
One of life insurance's most important benefits is that it is not considered part of the estate of the policy holder. The death benefit that is paid by the insurance company goes exclusively to the beneficiaries listed on the policy. This shields the proceeds of the policy from fees and costs that can reduce an estate, including probate proceedings, attorneys' fees and claims made by creditors. The distribution of your life insurance policy is also unaffected by delays of the estate's distribution, like probate. Your beneficiaries will get the proceeds of the policy in a timely fashion, regardless of how long it takes for the rest of your estate to be settled.

Investing a portion of your assets in a life insurance policy can also protect that portion of your estate from creditors. If you owe money to someone or some entity at the time of your death, a creditor is not able to claim any money from a life insurance policy or an annuity, for that matter. As an exception to this rule, if you had already used the life insurance policy as collateral against a loan. If a large portion of the money you want to dedicate to your legacy is sitting in a savings account, investment or other liquid form, creditors may be able to receive their claim on it before your beneficiaries get anything, that is if there's anything left. A life insurance policy protects your assets from creditors and ensures that your beneficiaries get the money that you intend them to have.

HOW MUCH LIFE INSURANCE DO YOU NEED?
Determining the type of policy and the amount right for you depends on an analysis of your needs. A financial professional

can help you complete a needs analysis that will highlight the amount of insurance that you require to meet your goals. This type of personalized review will allow you to determine ways to continue providing income for your spouse or any dependents you may have. A financial professional can also help you calculate the amount of income that your policy should replace to meet the needs of your beneficiaries and the duration of the distribution of that income.

You may also want to use your life insurance policy to meet any expenses associated with your death. These can include funeral costs, fees from probate and legal proceedings, and taxes. You may also want to dedicate a portion of your policy proceeds to help fund tuition or other expenses for your children or grandchildren. You can buy a policy and hope it covers all of those costs, or you can work with a professional who can calculate exactly how much insurance you need and how to structure it to meet your goals. Which would you rather do?

AVOIDING POTENTIAL SNAGS

There are benefits to having life insurance supersede the direction given in a will or other estate plan, but there are also some potential snags that you should address to meet your wishes. For example, if your will instructs that your assets be divided equally between your two children but your life insurance beneficiary is listed as just one of the children, the assets in the life insurance policy will only be distributed to the child listed as the beneficiary. The beneficiary designation of your life insurance supersedes your will's instruction. This is important to understand when designating beneficiaries on a policy you purchase. Work with a professional to make sure that your beneficiaries are accurately listed on your assets, especially your life insurance policies.

USING LIFE INSURANCE TO BUILD YOUR LEGACY

Depending on your goals, there are strategies you can use that could multiply how much you leave behind. Life insurance is one of the most surefire and efficient investment tools for building a substantial legacy that will meet your financial goals.

Here is a brief overview of how life insurance can boost your legacy:

- Life insurance provides an immediate increase in your legacy.
- It provides an income tax-advantaged death benefit for your beneficiaries.
- A good life insurance policy has the opportunity to accumulate value over time.
- It may have an option to include long-term care (LTC) or chronic illness benefits should you require them.

If your Safe Money income needs for retirement are met, you may have extra assets that you want to earmark as legacy funds. By electing to invest those assets into a life insurance policy, you can immediately increase the amount of your legacy. Remember, **life insurance allows you to transfer a tax-advantaged lump sum of money to your beneficiaries. It remains in your control during your lifetime, can provide for your long-term care needs and bypasses probate costs.** And make no mistake, taxes can have a huge impact on your legacy. Not only that, income and assets from your legacy can have tax implications for your beneficiaries, as well.

Here's a brief overview of how taxes could affect your legacy and your beneficiaries:

- The higher your income, the higher the rate at which it is taxed.
- Withdrawals from qualified plans are taxed as income.

- What's more, when you leave a large qualified plan, it ends up being taxed at a high rate.
- If you left a $500,000 IRA to your child, they could end up owing as much as $140,000 in income taxes.
- However, if you could just withdraw $50,000 a year, the tax bill might only be $10,000 per year.

How could you use that annual amount to leave a larger legacy? Luckily, you can leverage a life insurance policy to avoid those tax penalties, preserving a larger amount of your legacy and freeing your beneficiaries from an added tax burden.

> *When Hannah turned 70 years old, she decided it was time to look into life insurance policy options. She still feels young, but she remembers that her mother died in early 70s, and she wants to plan ahead so she can pass on some of her legacy to her grandchildren just like her grandmother did for her.*

> *Hannah doesn't really want to think about life insurance, but she does want the security, reliability and tax-advantaged distribution that it offers. She lives modestly, and her Social Security benefit meets most of her income needs. As the beneficiary of her late husband's Certificate of Deposit (CD), she has $100,000 in an account that she has never used and doesn't anticipate ever needing since her income needs were already met.*

> *After looking at several different investment options with a professional, Hannah decides that a Single Premium life insurance policy fits her needs best. She can buy the policy with a $100,000 one-time payment and she is guaranteed that it would provide more than the value of the contract to her beneficiaries. If she left the money in the CD, it would be subject to taxes. But for every dollar that she puts into the*

*life insurance policy, her beneficiaries are guaranteed at least that dollar plus a death benefit, and all of it will be **tax-free!***

For $100,000, Hannah's particular policy offers a $170,000 death benefit distribution to her beneficiaries. By moving the $100,000 from a CD to a life insurance policy, Hannah increases her legacy by 70 percent. Not only that, she has also sheltered it from taxes, so her beneficiaries will be able to receive $1.70 for every $1.00 that she entered into the policy! While buying the policy doesn't allow her to use the money for herself, it does allow her family to benefit from her well-planned legacy.

MAKE YOUR WISHES KNOWN

Estate taxes used to be a much hotter topic in the mid-2000s when the estate tax limits and exclusions were much smaller and taxed at a higher rate than today. In 2008, estates valued at $2 million or more were taxed at 45 percent. Just two years later, the limit was raised to $5 million dollars taxed at 35 percent. The limit has continued to rise ever since. The limit applies to fewer people than before. Estate organization, however, is just as important as ever, and it affects everyone.

Ask yourself:

- Are your assets actually titled and held the way you think they are?
- Are your beneficiaries set up the way you think they should be?
- Have there been changes to your family or those you desire as beneficiaries?

There is more to your legacy beyond your property, money, investments and other assets that you leave to family members, loved ones and charities. Everyone has a legacy beyond money. You also leave behind personal items of importance, your values and beliefs, your personal and family history, and your wishes. Beyond a will and a plan for your assets, it is important that you make your wishes known to someone for the rest of your personal legacy. When it comes time for your family and loved ones to make decisions after you are gone, knowing your wishes can help them make decisions that honor you and your legacy, and give meaning to what you leave behind. Your professional can help you organize.

Think about your:
- Personal stories / recollections
- Values
- Personal items of emotional significance
- Financial assets

Do you want to make a plan to pass these things on to your family?

WORKING WITH A PROFESSIONAL

Part of using life insurance to your greatest advantage is selecting the policy and provider that can best meet your goals. Venturing into the jungle of policies, brokers and salespeople can be overwhelming, and can leave you wondering if you've made the best decision. Working with a trusted financial professional can help you cut through the red tape, the "sales-speak" and confusion to find a policy that meets your goals and best serves your desires for your money. If you already have a policy, a financial professional can help you review it and become familiar with the policy's premium, the guarantees the policy affords, its performance, and its features and benefits. A financial professional can also help you make any necessary changes to the policy.

> *» When Maggie turned 88, her daughter finally convinced her to meet with a financial professional to help her organize her assets and get her legacy in order. Although Maggie is*

reluctant to let a stranger in on her personal finances, she ends up very glad that she did.

In the process of listing Maggie's assets and her beneficiaries, her professional finds a man's name listed as the beneficiary of an old life insurance annuity that she owns. It turns out, the man is Maggie's ex-husband who is still alive. Had Maggie passed away before her ex-husband, the annuities and any death benefits that came with them, would have been passed on to her ex-husband. This does not reflect her latest wishes.

Things change, relationships evolve and the way you would like your legacy organized needs to adapt to the changes that happen throughout your life. There may be a new child or grandchild in your family, or you may have been divorced or remarried. A professional will regularly review your legacy assets and ask you questions to make sure that everything is up to date and that the current organization reflects your current wishes.

CHAPTER 12 RECAP //

- Legacy planning tools include the creation of wills, trusts, living wills, and durable power of attorney for health care considerations. An estate planning attorney can help you with your individual needs.
- Review your current life insurance policies in order to determine if refinancing your life insurance makes sense.
- Life insurance provides for the distribution of tax-free, liquid assets to your beneficiaries and can significantly build your legacy. They can also provide Living Benefits to help you pay for the high costs of medical care while you are still living.
- Working with a financial professional can help you select the policy that best meets your needs, or can help you fine tune your existing policy to better reflect your desires and intentions.

13

CHOOSING A FINANCIAL PROFESSIONAL

From the moment you dip your toes into the retirement planning pool to the point you start swimming laps, your assets organized, your income needs met, and your accumulation and legacy plans in place, working with a professional that you trust can make all the difference in how well your retirement reflects your desires.

It is important to know what you are looking for before taking the plunge. There are many people that would love to handle your money, but not everyone is qualified to handle it in a way that leads to a holistic approach to creating a solid retirement plan.

The distinction being made here is that you should look for someone that puts your interests first and actively wants to help you meet your goals and objectives. Oftentimes, the products someone sells you matter less than their dedication to making sure that you have a plan that meets your needs.

Professionals take your whole financial position into consideration. They make plans that adjust your risk exposure, invest in tools that secure your desired income during retirement and create investment strategies that allow you to continue accumulating wealth during your retirement for you to use later or to contribute to your legacy. If you buy stocks with a broker, use a different agent for a life insurance policy and have an unmanaged 401(k) through your employer, working with a financial professional will consolidate the management of your assets so you have one trustworthy person quarterbacking all of the team elements of your portfolio. Financial products and investment tools change, but the concepts that lie behind wise retirement planning are lasting. In the end, a financial professional's approach is designed for those serious about planning for retirement. *Can you say the same thing about the person that advises you about your financial life?*

It's easy to see how choosing a financial professional can be one of the most important decisions you can make in your life. Not only do they provide you with advice, they also manage the personal assets that supply your retirement income and contribute to your legacy. So, how do you find a good one?

HOW TO FIND A FINANCIAL PROFESSIONAL YOU CAN TRUST

Taking care to select a financial professional is one of the best things you can do for yourself and for your future. Your professional has influence and control of your investment decisions, making their role in your life more than just important. Your financial security and the quality of your retirement depends on the decisions, investment strategies and asset structuring that you and your professional create.

Working with a professional is different than calling up a broker when you want to buy or trade some stock. This isn't a decision that you can hand off to anyone else. You need to bring your time and attention to the table when it comes to finding someone with whom you can entrust your financial life. Separating the wheat from the chaff will take some work, but you'll be happy you did it.

While no one can tell you exactly who to choose or how to choose them, the following information can help you narrow the field:

You can start by asking your friends, family and colleagues for referrals. You will want to pay particular attention to the recommendations that you get from others who are in your similar financial situation and who have similar lifestyle choices. The professional for the CEO of your company may have a different skill-set than the skill-set of the professional befitting your cousin who has 3 kids and a Subaru like you. Do follow-up research on the Internet as well. Look up the people who have been recommended to you on websites like LinkedIn that show the work history, referrals and experience of the candidates that you find most attractive. You will also learn about the firms with or for whom they work. The investment philosophies and reputations of the companies they work for will tell you a lot about how they will handle your money.

The other side of the coin, however, is that everyone and their brother has a recommendation about how you should manage your money and who should manage it for you. From hot stock tips to "the best money manager in the state," people love to share good information that makes them look like they are in-the-know. Nobody wants to talk about the bad stock purchases they made, the times they lost money and the poor selections they made regarding financial professionals or stock brokers. If you decide to take a friend or family member's recommendation, make sure they have a substantial, long-term experience with the financial professional and that their glowing review isn't just based on a one-time "win."

You can also use online tools like the search function of the Financial Planning Association (http://www.fpanet. org/) and the National Association of Personal Financial professionals (http://www.napfa.org/). Most of the professionals listed on these sites do not earn commissions from selling financial products, but are instead paid on a fee-only basis for their services. It is important to understand how your professional is being paid. It is generally considered preferable to work with a fee-based professional who will not have conflicts of interests between earning a commission and acting in your best interests.

Many professionals may also be brokers or dealers that can earn commissions on things like life insurance, certain types of annuities and disability insurance. These professionals have most likely intentionally overlapped their roles so that if their clients choose to purchase insurance or investment products that require a broker or dealer, those clients won't have to find an additional person to work with. Again, understanding the role of your professional will help you make your determination.

NARROWING THE FIELD

1. Decide on the Type of Professional with Whom You Want to Work. There are four basic kinds of financial professionals. Many professionals may play overlapping roles. It is important to know a professional's primary function, how they charge for their services and whether they are obligated to act in your best interest.

Registered representatives, better known as stockbrokers or bank / investment representatives, make their living by earning commissions on insurance products and investment services. Stockbrokers basically sell you things. The products from which they make the highest commission are sometimes the products that they recommend to their clients. If you want to make a simple transaction, such as buying or selling a particular stock, a registered representative can help you. Although registered representatives are licensed professionals, if you want to create a structured and planful approach to positioning your assets for retirement, you might want to consider continuing your search.

The term "planner" is often misused. It can refer to credible professionals that are CPAs, CFPs and ChFCs to your uncle's next door neighbor who claims to have a lead on some undervalued stock about to be "discovered." A wide array of people may claim to be planners because there are no requirements to be a planner. The term financial planner, however, refers to someone who is properly registered as an investment advisor and serves as a fiduciary as described below.

Financial professionals are the diamonds in the rough. These Registered Investment Advisors are compensated on a fee basis. They do, however, often have licensure as stockbrokers or insurance agents, allowing them to earn commissions on certain transactions. More importantly, **financial professionals are financial fiduciaries, meaning they are required to make financial decisions in your best interest and reflecting your risk tolerance.** Investment Advisors are held to high ethical standards and are highly regarded in the financial industry. Financial professionals also often take a more comprehensive approach to asset management. These professionals are trained and credentialed to plan and coordinate their clients' assets in order to meet their goals or retirement and legacy planning. They are not focused on individual stocks, investments or markets. They look at the big picture, the whole enchilada.

Money managers are on par with financial professionals. However, they are often given explicit permission to make investment decisions without advanced approval by their clients.

Understanding who you are working with and what their title is the first step to planning your retirement. While each of the above-mentioned types of financial professionals can help you with aspects of your finances, it is **financial professionals** who have the most intimate role, the most objective investment strategies and the most unbiased mode of compensation for their services. A financial professional can also help you with the non-financial aspects of your legacy and can help you find ways to create a tax planning strategy to help you save money.

2. Be Objective. At the end of the day, you need to separate the weak from the strong. While you might want a strong personal rapport with your professional, or you may want to choose your professional for their personality and positive attitude, it is more important that you find someone who will give sage advice regarding achieving your retirement goals.

It can be helpful to use a process of elimination to narrow the field of potential professionals. Look into five or six potential leads and cross off your list the ones that don't meet your requirements until only one or two remain. Cross-check your remaining choices against the list of things you need from a professional. Make sure they represent a firm that has the investment tools and products that you desire, and make sure they have experience in retirement planning. That is, after all, the main goal.

Don't be afraid to investigate each of your candidates. You'll want to ask the same questions and look for the same information from everyone you consider so you can then compare them and discern which is best for you. You'll want to take a look at the specific credentials of each professional, their experience and competence, their ethics and fiduciary status, their history and track record, and a list of the services that they offer. The professionals who meet all or most of your qualifications are the ones you will contact for an interview.

Potential professionals should meet your qualifications in the following categories:

Credentials: Look at their experience, the quality of their education, any associations to which they belong and certifications they have earned. Someone who has continued their professional education through ongoing certifications will be more up-to-date on current financial practices compared to someone who got their degree 25 years ago and hasn't done a thing since.

Practices: Look at the track record of your candidates, how they are compensated for their services, the reports and analysis they offer, and their value added services.

Services: Your professional must meet your needs. If you are planning your retirement, you should work with someone who offers services that help you to that end. You want someone who can offer planning, advice on investment strategies, ways to calculate risk, advice on insurance and annuities products, and ways to manage your tax strategy.

Ethics: You want to work with someone who is above board and does things the right way. Vet them by checking their compliance record, current licensing, fiduciary status and, yes, even their criminal record. You never know!

3. Ask for and Check References. Once you have selected two or three professionals that you want to meet, call or email them and ask for references. Every professional should be able to provide you with at least two or three names. In fact, they will probably be eager to share them with you. Most professionals rely on references for validation of their success, quality of services and likability. You should, however, take them with a grain of salt. You have no way to know whether or not references are a professional's friends or colleagues.

It is worth contacting references, however, to check for inconsistencies. Ask each reference the same set of questions to get the same basic information. How long have they been working with the professional? What kind of services have they used and were they happy with them? What type of financial planning did they use the professional for? Were they versed in the type of financial planning that you needed? You can also ask them direct questions to elicit candid responses. What was the full cost of the expenses that your professional charged you? Do the reports and statements you receive come from the same firm? Questions like these can help you get a sense of how well the reference knows their professional and whether or not they are a quality reference.

A good reference is a bit like icing on the cake. It's nice to have them, but nothing speaks louder than a good track record and quality experience. And remember that a good reference, while nice to hear, is relatively cheap. How many times have you heard someone on the golf course or at work telling you how great their stockbroker is? But how many times have you heard about the bad investments or losses they have experienced?

4. Use the Internet. As a final step before picking up the phone and calling your candidates, do some digging to discover if anyone on your list has a history of unlawful or unethical practices, or has been disciplined for any of their professional behavior or decisions. Don't worry, you don't have to hire a private investigator. You can easily find this information on the Financial Industry Regulatory Authority's (FINRA) online BrokerCheck tool: http://www.finra.org/Investors/ToolsCalculators/BrokerCheck/.

You should obviously explore the website of a potential professional and the website of the firm that they represent. The Internet allows you to go beyond the online business card of a professional to gain access to information that they don't control. It may all be good information! Or a brief search of the Internet could reveal a sketchy past. The best part is that the Internet allows you to find helpful information in an anonymous fashion.

Start with Google (www.google.com) and search the name of a potential professional and their firm. Keep your eyes trained on third party sources such as articles, blog posts or news stories that mention the professional. You can also check a professional's compliance records online with the Financial Industry Regulatory Authority (FINRA) and the Securities and Exchange Commission (SEC). If you want to dig deeper, you can combine search terms like "scams," "lawsuits," "suspensions" and "fraud" with a professional's or firm's name to see what information arises. More likely than not, you won't find anything. But if you do, you'll be glad that you checked.

HOW TO INTERVIEW CANDIDATES

After vetting your candidates and narrowing down a list of professionals that you think might be a good fit for you, it's time to start interviewing.

When you meet in person with a professional, you want to take advantage of your time with them. The presentations and information that they share with you will be important to pay attention to, but you will also want to control some aspects of the interview. After a professional has told you what they want you to hear, it's time to ask your own questions to get the specific information you need to make your decision.

Make sure to prepare a list of questions and an informal agenda so that you can keep track of what you want to ask and what points you want the professional to touch on during the interview. Using the same questions and agenda will also allow you to more easily compare the professionals after you have interviewed them all. Remember that these interviews are just that, *interviews*. You are meeting with several professionals to determine with whom you want to work. Don't agree to anything or sign anything during an interview until after you have made your final decision.

It can also be helpful to put a time limit on your interviews and to meet the professionals at their offices. The time limit will keep things on track and will allow structured time for presentations and questions/discussion. By meeting them at their office, you can get a sense of the work environment, the staff culture and attitude, and how the firm does business. If you are unable to travel to a professional's office and must meet them at your home or office, make sure that your interviews are scheduled with plenty of time between so the professionals don't cross each other's paths.

You can use the following questions during an initial interview to get an understanding of how each professional does business and whether they are a good fit for you:

1. How do you charge for your services? How much do you charge? This information should be easy to find on their website, but if you don't see it, ask. Find out if they charge an initial planning fee, if they charge a percentage for assets under their management and if they make money by selling specific financial products or services. If so, you should follow up by asking how much the service costs. This will give you an idea of how they really make their money and if they have incentive to sell certain products over others. Make sure you understand exactly how you will be charged so there are no surprises down the road if you decide to work with this person.

2. What are your credentials, licenses, and certifications? There are Certified Financial Planners (CFPs), Chartered Financial Consultants (ChFCs), Investment Advisor Representatives, Certified Public Accountants (CPAs) and Personal Financial Specialists (PFSs). Whatever their credentials or titles, you want to be sure that the professional you work with is an expert in the field relevant to your circumstances. If you want someone to manage your money, you will most likely look for an Investment Advisor. Someone that works with an independent firm will likely have a team of CPAs, CFPs and other financial experts upon whom they can draw. If you like the professional you are meeting with and you think they might be a good fit, but they don't have the accounting experience you want them to have, ask about their firm and the resources available to them. If they work closely with CPAs that are experienced in your needs, it could be a good match.

3. What are the financial services that you and your firm provide? The question within the question here is, "Can you help me achieve my goals?" Some people can only provide you with investment advice, and others are tax consultants. You will likely want to work with someone that provides a complete suite of financial planning services and products that touch on retirement planning, insurance options, legacy and estate structuring, and tax planning. Whatever services they provide, make sure they meet your needs and your anticipated needs.

4. What kinds of clients do you work with the most? A lot of financial professionals work within a niche: retirement planning, risk assessment, life insurance, etc. Finding someone who works with other people that are in the same financial boat as you and who have similar goals can be an important way to make sure they understand your needs. While someone might be a crackerjack annuities cowboy, you might not be interested in that option. Ask follow-up questions that will really help you understand where their expertise lies and whether or not their experience lines up with your needs.

5. May I see a sample of one of your financial plans? You wouldn't buy a car without test driving it, and you should not work with a professional without seeing a sample of how they do business. While there is no formal structure that a financial plan has to follow, the variation between professionals can help you find someone who "speaks your language." One professional may provide you with an in-depth analysis that relies heavily on info graphics and diagrams. Someone else may give you a seven page review of your assets and general recommendations. By seeing a sample plan, you can narrow down who presents information in the way that you desire and in ways that you understand.

6. How do you approach investing? You may be entirely in the dark about how to approach your investments, or you might have some guiding principles. Either way, ask each candidate what their philosophy is. Some will resonate with you and some won't. A good professional who has a realistic approach to investing won't promise you the moon or tell you that they can make you a lot of money. Professionals who are successful at retirement planning and full service financial management will tell you that they will listen to your goals, risk tolerance and comfort level with different types of investment strategies. Working with someone that you trust is critical, and this question in particular can help you find out who you can and who you can't.

7. How do you remain in contact with your clients? Does your prospective professional hold annual, quarterly or monthly meetings? How often do *you* want to meet with your professional? Some people want to check in once a year, go over everything and make sure their ducks are all in a row. If any changes over the previous year or additions to their legacy planning strategy came up, they'll do it on that date. Other people want a monthly update to be more involved in the decision making process and to understand what's happening with their portfolio. You basically need to determine the right degree of involvement for both you and your financial professional. You'll also want to feel out how your professional communicates. Do you prefer phone calls or face-to-face meetings? Do you want your professional to explain things to you in detail or to summarize for you what decisions they've made? Is the professional willing to give you their direct phone number or their email address? More importantly, do you want that information and do you want to be able to contact them in those ways?

8. Are you my main contact, or do you work with a team? This is another way of finding out how involved with you your professional will be, and how often they will meet with you. It is also a way to discover how the firm they represent operates and manages their clients. Some professionals will answer their own phone, meet with you regularly and have your home phone number on speed dial. Others will meet with you once a year and have a partner or assistant check in with you every quarter to give you an update. Other companies take an entirely team-based approach whereby clients have a main contact but their portfolio is handled by a team of professionals that represent the firm. One way isn't better than another, but one way will be best for you. Find out how the professional you are interviewing operates before entering into an agreement.

9. How do you provide a unique experience for your clients? This is a polite way of asking, "Why should I work with you?" A professional should have a compelling answer to this question that connects with you. Their answer will likely touch on their investment philosophy, their communication style and their expertise. If you hear them describing strengths and philosophies that resonate with you, keep them on your list. Some professionals will tell you that they will make investments with your money that match your values, others will say they will maximize your returns and others will say they will protect your capital while structuring your assets for income. Whatever you're looking for in a professional, you will most likely find it in the answer to this question.

This last question you will want to ask *yourself* after you've met with someone who you are considering hiring:

10. Did they ask questions and show signs that they were interested in working with me? A professional who will structure your assets to reflect your risk tolerance and to position you for a comfortable retirement must be a good listener. You will want to pass by a professional who talks non-stop and tells you what to do without listening to what you want them to do. If you felt they listened well and understood your needs, and seemed interested and experienced in your situation, then they might be right for you.

THE IMPORTANCE OF INDEPENDENCE

Not all investment firms and financial professionals are created equal. The information in this book has systematically shown that leveraging investments for income and accumulation in today's market requires new ideas and modern planning. In short, you need innovative ideas to come up with the creative solutions that will provide you with the retirement that you want. Innovation thrives on independence. No matter how good a financial professional is, the firm that they represent needs to operate on principles that make sense in today's economy. Remember, advice about money has been around forever. Good advice, however, changes with the times.

Timing the market, relying on the sale of stocks for income and banking on high treasury and bond returns are not strategies. They aren't even realistic ways to make money or to generate income. Working with an independent agent can help you break free from the old ways of thinking and position you to create a realistic retirement plan.

Working with an independent professional who relies on fee-based income tied to the success of their performance will also give you greater peace of mind. When you do well, they do well, and that's the way it should be. Your independent financial professional will make sure that:

- Your assets are organized and structured to reflect your risk tolerance.
- Your assets will be available to you when you need them and in the way that you need them.
- You will have a lifetime income that will support your lifestyle through your retirement.
- You are handling your taxes as efficiently as possible.
- Your legacy is in order.
- Your Risk Money is turned into Safe Money.

» Remember Lee and Paula from Chapter 1? Even though they knew they had Social Security benefits coming, they placed some money in savings and each had a pension or a 401(k). **Before they met with a financial professional, they had no idea what their retirement would look like.** *After their meeting, they began to think about their savings in terms of their ability to produce income. They identified the purpose of the money they had invested, understood how much those investments were worth and how they were positioned for risk. They also understood what risk really means: the amount of money they should be comfortable losing. Looking at their savings this way clarified what they wanted their money to do. They secured their principal first so it was guaranteed not to diminish. They put that money into multiple investment vehicles that could provide a steady stream of income so they could pay their bills every month from the moment they retired until the day they died. They maximized their Social Security benefit by targeting the year and month they would get the most lifetime benefits. Their professional also helped them make decisions that impacted their taxes,*

protecting the value of their assets and allowing them to keep more of their money in order to create their definition of a legacy.

This isn't a fairy tale scenario. This is an example of how much you stand to gain by meeting with a financial professional who can help you create a planful approach to your retirement. The concept of Risk Money and Safe Money didn't just apply to their money, it also applied to Lee and Paula. They hoped they had saved enough for retirement, but they didn't understand the amount of risk their assets were exposed to, or how they should be positioned in order to provide income. Working with a financial professional allowed them to secure their income needs for the rest of their lives and that gave them the peace of mind to enjoy the retirement they deserved.

Now, ask yourself: Is your retirement built on hopes and dreams, or a solid, predictable plan?

IT'S WORTH IT!

Finding, interviewing and selecting a financial professional can seem like a daunting task. And honestly, it will take a good amount of work to narrow the field and find the one you want. In the end, it is worth the blood, sweat and tears. Your retirement, lifestyle, assets and legacy is on the line. The choices you make today will have lasting impacts on your life and the life of your loved ones. Working with someone you trust and know you can rely on to make decisions that will benefit you is invaluable. The work it takes to find them is something you will never regret.

Here is a recap of why working with a financial professional is the best retirement decision you can make:

CHAPTER 13 RECAP //

- A good financial professional puts your needs first. Your risk tolerance, goals, objectives, needs, wants, liquidity concerns and timeline worries should be the focus of the meeting before they try to sell you any products. A plan is only good if it is a good fit for you and your family.

- Finding a financial professional you can trust is imperative, because money isn't just about numbers; it's about the life events and the people that come attached to those numbers.

- To find a professional you can trust, start by asking family and friends for referrals. Make sure to do your due diligence and check out the references of anyone who is recommended to you. Look for resources online such as the Financial Planning Association and the National Association of Personal Financial professionals.

- When interviewing candidates, make sure you understand how they charge for their services. Also look for credentials, licenses and certifications. Ask questions such as: How often do you check in with your clients? May I see a sample of one of your financial plans? And, How do you approach investing? These questions will help ensure that you and your professional are a good fit for each other.

GLOSSARY*

ANNUAL RESET *(ANNUAL RATCHET, CLIQUET)* – Crediting methods measuring index movement over a one year period. Positive interest is calculated and credited at the end of each contract year and cannot be lost if the index subsequently declines. Say that the index increased from 100 to 110 in one year and the indexed annuity had an 80 percent participation rate. The insurance company would take the 10 percent gross index gain for the year (110-100/100), apply the participation rate (10 percent index gain x 80 percent rate) and credit 8 percent interest to the annuity. But, what if in the following year the index declined back to 100? The individual would keep the 8 percent interest earned and simply receive zero interest for the down year. An annual reset structure

*"Glossary of Terms." FixedAnnuityFacts.com. NAFA, the National Association for Fixed Annuities, n.d. 12 Nov. 2013

preserves credited gains and treats negative index periods as years with zero growth.

ANNUITANT – The person, usually the annuity owner, whose life expectancy is used to calculate the income payment amount on the annuity.

ANNUITY – An annuity is a contract issued by an insurance company that often serves as a type of savings plan used by individuals looking for long term growth and protection of assets that will likely be needed within retirement.

AVERAGING – Index values may either be measured from a start point to an end point (point-to-point) or values between the start point and end point may be averaged to determine an ending value. Index values may be averaged over the days, weeks, months or quarters of the period.

BENEFICIARY – A beneficiary is the person designated to receive payments due upon the death of the annuity owner or the annuitant themselves.

BONUS RATE – A bonus rate is the "extra" or "additional" interest paid during the first year (the initial guarantee period), typically used as an added incentive to get consumers to select their annuity policy over another.

CALL OPTION *(ALSO SEE PUT OPTION)* – Gives the holder the right to buy an underlying security or index at a specified price on or before a given date.

CAP – The maximum interest rate that will be credited to the annuity for the year or period. The cap usually refers to the maximum interest credited after applying the participation rate or yield spread. If the index methodology showed a 20 percent increase, the participation rate was 60 percent and the maximum interest cap was 10 percent, the contract would credit 10 percent interest. A few annuities use a maximum gain cap instead of a maximum interest cap with the participation rate or yield spread applied to the lesser of the gain or the cap. If the index methodology showed a 20 percent increase, the participation rate was 60 percent and the maximum gain cap was 10 percent, the contract would credit 6 percent interest.

COMPOUND INTEREST – Interest is earned on both the original principal and on previously earned interest. It is more favorable than simple interest. Suppose that your original principal was $1 and your interest rate was 10 percent for five years. With simple interest, your value is ($1 + $0.10 interest each year) = $1.50. With compound interest, your value is ($1 x 1.10 x 1.10 x 1.10 x 1.10 x 1.10) = $1.61. The advantage of compound interest over simple interest becomes greater as each subsequent period passes.

CREDITING METHOD *(ALSO SEE METHODOLOGY)* – The formula(s) used to determine the excess interest that is credited above the minimum interest guarantee.

DEATH BENEFITS – The payment the annuity owner's estate or beneficiaries will receive if he or she dies before the annuity matures. On most annuities, this is equal to the current account value. Some annuities offer an enhanced value at death via an optional rider that has a monthly or annual fee associated with it.

EXCESS INTEREST – Interest credited to the annuity contract above the minimum guaranteed interest rate. In an indexed annuity the excess interest is determined by applying a stated crediting method to a specific index or indices.

FIXED ANNUITY – A contract issued by an insurance company guaranteeing a minimum interest rate with the crediting of excess interest determined by the performance of the insurer's general account. Index annuities are fixed annuities.

FIXED DEFERRED ANNUITY – With fixed annuities, an insurance company offers a guaranteed interest rate plus safety of your principal and earnings ((subject to the claims-paying ability of the insurance company). Your interest rate will be reset periodically, based on economic and other factors, but is guaranteed to never fall below a certain rate.

FREE WITHDRAWALS – Withdrawals that are free of surrender charges.

INDEX – The underlying external benchmark upon which the crediting of excess interest is based, also a measure of the prices of a group of securities.

IRA *(INDIVIDUAL RETIREMENT ACCOUNT)* – An IRA is a tax-advantaged personal savings plan that lets an individual set aside money for retirement. All or part of the participant's contributions may be tax deductible, depending on the type of IRA chosen and the participant's personal financial circumstances. Distributions from many employer-sponsored retirement plans may be eligible to be rolled into an IRA to continue tax-deferred growth until the funds are needed. An annuity can be used as an IRA; that is, IRA funds can be used to purchase an annuity.

IRA ROLLOVER – IRA rollover is the phrase used when an individual who has a balance in an employer-sponsored retirement plan transfers that balance into an IRA. Such an exchange, when properly handled, is a tax-advantaged transaction.

LIQUIDITY – The ease with which an asset is convertible to cash. An asset with high liquidity provides flexibility, in that the owner can easily convert it to cash at any time, but it also tends to decrease profitability.

MARKET RISK – The risk of the market value of an asset fluctuating up or down over time. In a fixed or fixed indexed annuity, the original principal and credited interest are not subject to market risk. Even if the index declines, the annuity owner would receive no less than their original principal back if they decided to cash in the policy at the end of the surrender period. Unlike a security, indexed annuities guarantee the original premium and the premium is backed by, and is as safe as, the insurance company that issued it (subject to the claims-paying ability of the insurance company).

METHODOLOGY *(ALSO SEE CREDITING METHOD)* – The way that interest crediting is calculated. On fixed indexed annuities, there are a variety of different methods used to determine how index movement becomes interest credited.

MINIMUM GUARANTEED RETURN *(MINIMUM INTEREST RATE)* – Fixed indexed annuities typically provide a minimum guaranteed return over the life of the contract. At the time that the owner chooses to terminate the contract, the cash surrender value is compared to a second value calculated using the minimum guaranteed return and the higher of the two values is paid to the annuity owner.

OPTION – A contract which conveys to its holder the right, but not the obligation, to buy or sell something at a specified price on or before a given date. After this given date the option ceases to exist. Insurers typically buy options to provide for the excess interest potential. Options may be American style whereby they may be exercised at any time prior to the given date, or they may have to be exercised only during a specified window. Options that may only be exercised during a specified period are European-style options.

OPTION RISK – Most insurers create the potential for excess interest in an indexed annuity by buying options. Say that you could buy a share of stock for $50. If you bought the stock and it rose to $60 you could sell it and net a $10 profit. But, if the stock price fell to $40 you'd have a $10 loss. Instead of buying the actual stock, we could buy an option that gave us the right to buy the stock for $50 at any time over the next year. The cost of the option is $2. If the stock price rose to $60 we would exercise our option, buy the stock at $50 and make $10 (less the $2 cost of the option). If the price of the stock fell to $40, $30 or $10, we wouldn't use the option and it would expire. The loss is limited to $2 – the cost of the option.

PARTICIPATION RATE – The percentage of positive index movement credited to the annuity. If the index methodology determined that the index increased 10 percent and the indexed annuity participated in 60 percent of the increase, it would be said that the contract has a 60 percent participation rate. Participation rates may also be expressed as asset fees or yield spreads.

POINT-TO-POINT – A crediting method measuring index movement from an absolute initial point to the absolute end point for a period. An index had a period starting value of 100 and a period ending value of 120. A point-to-point method would record a positive index movement of 20 [120-100] or a 20 percent positive movement [(120-100)/100]. Point-to-point usually refers to annual periods; however the phrase is also used instead of term end point to refer to multiple year periods.

PREMIUM BONUS – A premium bonus is additional money that is credited to the accumulation account of an annuity policy under certain conditions.

PUT OPTION *(ALSO SEE CALL OPTION)* – Gives the holder the right to sell an underlying security or index at a specified price on or before a given date.

QUALIFIED ANNUITIES *(QUALIFIED MONEY)* – Qualified annuities are annuities purchased for funding an IRA, 403(b) tax-deferred annuity or other type of retirement arrangements. An IRA or qualified retirement plan provides the tax deferral. An annuity contract should be used to fund an IRA or qualified retirement plan to benefit from an annuity's features other than tax deferral, including the safety features, lifetime income payout option and death benefit protection.

REQUIRED MINIMUM DISTRIBUTION *(RMD)* – The amount of money that Traditional, SEP and SIMPLE IRA owners and qualified plan participants must begin distributing from their retirement accounts by April 1 following the year they reach age 70.5. RMD amounts must then be distributed each subsequent year.

RETURN FLOOR – Another way of saying minimum guaranteed return.

ROTH IRA – Like other IRA accounts, the Roth IRA is simply a holding account that manages your stocks, bonds, annuities, mutual funds and CD's. However, future withdrawals (including earnings and interest) are typically tax-advantaged once the account has been open for five years and the account holder is age 59.5.

RULE OF 72 – Tells you approximately how many years it takes a sum to double at a given rate. It's handy to be able to figure out, without using a calculator, that when you're earning a 6 percent return, for example, by dividing 6 percent into 72, you'll find that it takes 12 years for money to double. Conversely, if you know it took a sum twelve years to double you could divide 12 into 72 to determine the annual return (6 percent).

SIMPLE INTEREST *(ALSO SEE COMPOUND INTEREST)* – Interest is only earned on the principal balance.

SPLIT ANNUITY – A split annuity is the term given to an effective strategy that utilizes two or more different annuity products – one designed to generate monthly income and the other to restore the original starting principal over a set period of time.

STANDARD & POOR'S 500 *(S&P 500)* – The most widely used external index by fixed indexed annuities. Its objective is to be a benchmark to measure and report overall U.S. stock market performance. It includes a representative sample of 500 common stocks from companies trading on the New York Stock Exchange, American Stock Exchange, and NASDAQ National Market System. The index represents the price or market value of the underlying stocks and does not include the value of reinvested dividends of the underlying stocks.

STOCK MARKET INDEX – A report created from a type of statistical measurement that shows up or down changes in a specific financial market, usually expressed as points and as a percentage, in a number of related markets, or in an economy as a whole (i.e. S&P 500 or New York Stock Exchange).

SURRENDER CHARGE – A charge imposed for withdrawing funds or terminating an annuity contract prematurely. There is no industry standard for surrender charges, that is, each annuity product has its own unique surrender charge schedule. The charge is usually expressed as a percentage of the amount withdrawn prematurely from the contract. The percentage tends to decline over time, ultimately becoming zero.

TRADITIONAL IRA – See <u>IRA (Individual Retirement Account)</u>

TERM END POINT – Crediting methods measuring index movements over a greater timeframe than a year or two. The opposite of an annual reset method. Also referred to as a term point-to-point method. Say that the index value was at 100 on the first day of the period. If the calculated index value was at 150 at the end of the period the positive index movement would be 50 percent (150-100/100). The company would credit a percentage of this movement as excess interest. Index movement is calculated and interest credited at the end of the term and interim movements during the period are ignored.

TERM HIGH POINT *(HIGH WATER MARK)* – A type of term end point structure that uses the highest anniversary index level as the end point. Say that the index value was at 100 on the first day of the period, reached a value of 160 at the end of a contract year during the period, and ended the period at 150. A term high point method would use the 160 value – the highest contract anniversary point reached during the period, as the end point and the gross index gain would be 60 percent (160-100/100). The company would then apply a participation rate to the gain.

TERM YIELD SPREAD – A type of term end point structure which calculates the total index gain for a period, computes the annual compound rate of return deducts a yield spread from the annual rate of return and then recalculates the total index gain for the period based on the net annual rate. Say that an index increased from 100 to 200 by the end of a nine year period. This is the equivalent of an 8 percent compound annual interest rate. If the annuity had a 2 percent term yield spread this would be deducted from the annual interest rate (8 percent-2 percent) and the net rate would be credited to the contract (6 percent) for each of the nine years. Total index gain may also be computed by using the highest anniversary index level as the end point.

VARIABLE ANNUITY – A contract issued by an insurance company offering separate accounts invested in a wide variety of stocks and/or bonds. The investment risk is borne by the annuity owner. Variable annuities are considered securities and require appropriate securities registration.

1035 EXCHANGE – The 1035 exchange refers to the section of tax code that allows annuity owners the flexibility to exchange one annuity for another without incurring any immediate tax liabilities. This action is most often utilized when an annuity holder decides they want to upgrade an annuity to a more favorable one, but they do not want to activate unnecessary tax liabilities that would typically be encountered when surrendering an existing annuity contract.

401(K) ROLLOVER – See <u>IRA Rollover</u>